T0277167

Advance Praise

"In *Embodied Self Awakening*, Nityda Gessel extends her invaluable knowledge to you, the reader. She offers actionable steps for understanding and processing trauma that appreciate the very important connection between the body and the mind. I highly recommend this book."

—**Gregory Scott Brown**, MD, psychiatrist, mental health
writer, and author of *The Self-Healing Mind*

"Nityda Gessel has creatively and intelligently woven insights from Buddhist psychology, trauma theory, and Indigenous wisdom into an accessible guide. Anyone looking to deepen their spiritual path while engaging their psychological journey will find *Embodied Self Awakening* both practical and inspiring."

—**Kimberly Ann Johnson**, author of *Call of the Wild: How We
Heal Trauma, Awaken Our Own Power, and Use it For Good*

"In *Embodied Self Awakening*, Nityda Gessel offers something magical—a path to truly healing our pain. She does so by combining wisdom from the East and the West. Her magic is not just in the way she shares these two seemingly opposed approaches to healing, but in how she excavates the essential elements that make both approaches powerful and effective. The result is a truly holistic approach to trauma that encourages us to embrace both our darkness and our light. It is as powerful as the merging of Shiva and Shakti, the joining together of both consciousness and nature, which allows us to experience the fullness of our being—body, mind, and spirit. I know that many, many people will benefit from the magic of this book and the alchemical brilliance that it holds."

—**Jivana Heyman**, author of *Accessible Yoga* and *Yoga Revolution*

"Nityda Gessel is a thoughtful, grounded, and wise guide. In this book she manages to connect the most cutting-edge trauma research with ancient and Indigenous wisdom in a way that brings to life some of the most important tools and perspectives for healing. Her writing is accessible and generous, and she takes the reader on an embodied journey that will no doubt profoundly touch anyone who picks up this book."

—**Hala Khouri**, MA, SEP, E-RYT, author of *Peace from Anxiety: Get Grounded, Build Resilience, and Stay Connected Amidst the Chaos*

EMBODIED
SELF
AWAKENING

EMBODIED
SELF
AWAKENING

Somatic Practices for Trauma Healing
and Spiritual Evolution

Nityda Gessel

W. W. NORTON & COMPANY
Celebrating a Century of Independent Publishing

Note to Readers. This book is intended as a general informational resource. The approaches and techniques described in this book are meant to supplement—and not to be a substitute for—professional care or treatment, and readers should consult with a qualified professional before embarking on any new physical, yoga, or breathwork regimen. No technique or recommendation is guaranteed to be safe or effective in all circumstances, and neither the publisher nor the author can guarantee the efficacy or appropriateness of any particular recommendation in every respect. The names and potentially identifying characteristics of patients described in this book have been changed and some are composites.

Any URLs displayed in this book link or refer to websites that existed as of press time. The publisher is not responsible for, and should not be deemed to endorse or recommend, any website, app, or other content that it did not create. The author also is not responsible for any third-party material.

Images in this book are courtesy of Tina Taylor (https://www.gentlelotus.studio/).

Frontis © asantosg / iStockPhoto.com
Chapter openers © cienpies / iStockPhoto.com
Text ornament © Sunny Universe / iStockPhoto.com

For information about permission to reproduce selections from this book, write to
Permissions, W. W. Norton & Company, Inc., 500 Fifth Avenue, New York, NY 10110

For information about special discounts for bulk purchases, please contact
W. W. Norton Special Sales at specialsales@wwnorton.com or 800-233-4830

Manufacturing by Lake Book Manufacturing
Book design by Anna Knighton
Production manager: Gwen Cullen

ISBN: 978-1-324-02005-9

W. W. Norton & Company, Inc., 500 Fifth Avenue, New York, NY 10110
www.wwnorton.com

W. W. Norton & Company Ltd., 15 Carlisle Street, London W1D 3BS

1 2 3 4 5 6 7 8 9 0

For Asha.
May you never forget
that you are already free.

Contents

Acknowledgments

I am only as strong as the ones who hold me.

With love and adoration . . .

I extend gratitude to my ancestors, for your vision, your enduring spirit, your voice, your legacy gifts—I truly felt your guidance and nurturing presence throughout each stage of this creative process.

Gratitude to Tina Taylor and your resolute devotion to the Trauma-Conscious Yoga Institute, and for sharing your talents and creating the beautiful images in this book (https://www.gentlelotus.studio/). Thank you for your upbeat positivity and vibrance, always.

Thank you to my support team at the Trauma-Conscious Yoga Institute. Tosha, Elizabeth, and the TA team, I could never have completed this book without you.

I'm grateful for my spiritual community of teachers and friends, and to my sangha at Tara Mandala. Gratitude to my fellow internal family systems folx—my teachers, colleagues, and friends within the IFS community that have inspired me to explore and make this model accessible.

Major thanks to Deborah Malmud, Mariah Eppes, and the Norton team for your devoted support and flexibility along this creative journey.

I bow to those who have been and are existing therapy clients: for your trust and willingness to live, to thrive, to blossom; conjuring up the courage to go to the dark, unvisited crevices of your being and navigate toward truth. Thank you for sharing your stories, your pain, your joys, and your victories—for stretching me and inspiring me to hold presence, to continue to do my own work. You are some of my greatest teachers.

Ryan, thank you for your steadiness—grounded in your expressions of patience, acceptance, courage and love. For the container of devotion you built around us and our family that allowed me the space to go inward, manifest, create, and see this vision out to fruition. To my sweet baby girl, Asha. You are a teacher by example, exemplifying what it means to show up fully and unapologetically as oneself; with fearlessness about taking up space and shining bright. You are freedom embodied. You inspired this work.

Foreword

Your energy introduces you before you even speak.

—MAYA ANGELOU

When I read these precious and beautiful words from Maya Angelou, they always remind me of my dear friend and amazing colleague, Nityda Gessel. They are a reminder to me that our healing is not separate from those we hold space for, but that we do have a responsibility to tend to our nervous systems with care and compassion so we can cultivate a safe and trauma-informed container for all those who have trusted us with their hearts. As Nityda so breathtakingly reminds us in the journey of her book, "there is no need to rush off toward enlightenment before we've done the work to care for our own shadows." She takes us on a deep, spiritual journey where there are no quick fixes, lists, or shortcuts. Instead, there is a gentle presence that compassionately invites us to tend to our pain with compassion and grace. She empowers us to follow the unique pace of our own nervous systems and find our pathway to embodied ease. She gives us permission to connect to our joy. She reminds us that we are worthy of gentleness, softness, and space in the healing process and reminds us to pour into ourselves, the way we so freely pour into others. She shines a light on the healing path and helps us see and uncover our own radiance.

I still remember traveling to Austin from Los Angeles to attend Nityda's Four-Day Trauma-Conscious Yoga Certification Training. I was coming at a particularly tender time where I had been overscheduled, overextended, exhausted, and living in survival mode for longer than I would like to admit. I felt deeply called to attend her training and share space with her, and I knew that even amid all of the barriers to getting there, I would make it happen. Everything in my body was telling me that I needed to go. I arrived late, rushing in with my coffee in hand, and immediately felt at ease when I found my space in the yoga studio, in the beautiful container she had created for the weekend. In the first few moments of hearing her speak, I felt both captivated and held. To witness another woman of color and trauma-informed yoga trainer in a field that is dominated by white male researchers stand in her truth and power was a deeply healing and affirming experience for me. That weekend I cried, laughed, rested, and could physically feel parts of myself that were softening and unfolding. She held space for the various intersections of my lived experience without ever making me feel like there was something wrong with me. Instead, she shined a light on the pieces that felt broken, and reminded me that I was inherently whole. She helped me remember that I was my own greatest teacher and that I could trust my needs and be reminded that those needs matter. We must never underestimate the power of reminding a survivor about the choices they have with their own bodies. The weekend left me speechless and broke my heart wide open. To now see her take her teachings pen to paper, where the entire world can access her magic is honestly the greatest gift. The world needs this healing now more than ever.

Just reading the pages of this book is a healing and transformative experience because they invite us into the full senses of our mind, body, and spirit. We cannot compartmentalize the way humans experience trauma, andnd we are worthy of teachers, healers, and practitioners who understand the impact that trauma has on the nervous system. Nityda is like a close companion, reminding us that we are never alone in our experience. She is there as a mirror in healing, helping us feel seen and enough; a steady and safe anchor, and a wise, embodied teacher who has walked the spiritual path of somatics and has turned her pain into medicine. She thoughtfully reminds us that we are worthy of releasing the grip and of giving our bodies the space they deserve to heal, exist, and be free.

Nityda reminds us that when we heal, we increase the capacity of our nervous system, which allows us to not be hijacked by what we have endured. Instead, we learn how to befriend all parts of ourselves. This is the journey towards radical self-compassion. Nityda's work is a reminder that you are worthy of your own healing, care, energy, time, and affection. Reading her own story in the book, which she so courageously shares with us, made me pause as the tears streamed down my face. I rested my palms over my heart and felt so much awe and gratitude for this woman, who has lit the pathway for those who can't see it themselves. Nityda weaves neuroscience, somatic psycho-therapy, Buddhist philosophy, an understanding of intergenerational and systemic trauma, somatic therapy skills, Indigenous African healing practices, social justice frameworks, Polyvagal Theory, and body-centered practices (yes, read all of that again) to create a com-prehensive and one-of-a-kind guide for all the brave souls who have opened themselves up to this journey.

The various intersections of Nityda's experience and practice as a woman of color, a healer, a mother, a trauma-informed yoga instruc-tor and trainer, and a somatic psychotherapist (just a few of the many incredible roles that she holds) allow her to be the perfect person to teach embodied self-awakening and fill a gap in the stories the world needs to hear and have access to. This book is a remembrance and an embodied path, reminding us that we are worthy of returning "home" to ourselves at our own pace. It is a reminder to stay curious about our pain and to give all parts of ourselves a "fair chance." This book will change and heal the lives of so many trauma survivors and healing practitioners. I am not the same person I was when I started this book. It has created little ripples of healing and pockets of awareness that have revealed themselves in their own time. What a gift.

Zahabiyah A. Yamasaki, MEd, RYT
author of *Trauma-Informed Yoga for Survivors of Sexual Assault: Practices for Healing and Teaching with Compassion* and Trauma-Informed Yoga Affirmation Card Deck

zabieyamasaki.com
IG: @transcending_trauma_with_yoga

Introduction

I invite you to press your feet into the earth, sitting or standing.

It doesn't matter where you are, outdoors or indoors. You are in the right place.

Releasing the tension from the feet, into the earth, I invite you to take a moment to consciously slow down. To pause. To be.

Take some time here.

Notice . . .

✳

What are you noticing?

A passing thought? Many thoughts?

Are there any feelings or emotions present right now?

Physical sensations?

There is no wrong or right here. No binary measure to determine your value or worthiness as a human. What you notice is what is . . . right now.

✳

Can you witness what is happening inside without turning away? Can you acknowledge what you witness inside, maybe even send it compassion, perhaps even gratitude, if it feels authentic?

There is no need to be here long. A single moment of inner inquiry is a step forward along your path.

So when it feels complete, soften your feet into the earth once more. And if your eyes were closed, take your time to blink them awake.

This book is an offering to be with, and to turn toward, that from which we instinctively retreat or pull away. We've learned how to push down our pain, deny its presence, mask it with a pill, or rush to move on. It's our survival instinct as survivors of trauma to run from or fight against that which ails us. Yet, when we fight against our internal turmoil, any glimmers of peace we experience are short lived. Pushing the pain away isn't a lasting solution because trauma is held in the body. We carry it with us. When we push the pain away and turn a blind eye to the suffering happening directly inside us, we miss out on the opportunity to get the most out of this precious life. We miss out on the joy and the freedom that comes with awakening.

Before we heal, when we look out into the world, what we see is our own trauma reflected back at us. When we heal, we begin to see things more clearly—we're not activated or hijacked by our nervous systems as easily, and we begin to feel more comfortable in our bodies, more at peace and more free in our lives. In my work as a somatic psychotherapist and yoga teacher, specializing in trauma healing, I've found again and again that the path of trauma healing and the path of spiritual evolution are one and the same.

When we make the choice to intentionally heal from the traumas of our past, we wake up to our true nature—who we are in our truth when we free ourselves from our conditioning and the aspects of our personality that were born from our wounds. Our true nature is who we are in the depths of our being, when we extract the pain and trauma of a dark, unpleasant past, whether our own or that of our ancestors. If we can make the choice to turn toward our pain and get to know it in a caring, compassionate way, liberation is on the other side.

Awakening is a heart-centered endeavor, one in which disembodiment is remedied as we reconnect our minds to our hearts. On this journey we lean in and get close to the parts of us that block self-compassion, befriending these parts and giving them what they need so that the burdens they've been carrying release organically. There is something in each of us that cannot be damaged by trauma, and it's this inner resource that is our greatest refuge and support along this healing journey.

I am in no way encouraging you to celebrate your trauma or saying that you should be wearing it like a badge of honor. That is contrary to what I am offering here. I am offering that since life brings joy yet also brings pain, we can allow our pain to alchemize us and help us become more free. Pain can be something we turn toward. Pain can be a portal for awakening.

THE APPROACH

This book is here to help you heal, awaken, and feel more free in your life. In this book I share the teachings and methods that have supported my own personal evolution, as well as those that have brought the most profound transformation to the psychotherapy clients I see. This book offers a bridge between East and West, marrying the wisdom of Buddhist psychology, yogic teachings, and Indigenous insights with somatic psychotherapy and modern neuroscience.

This book is meant to be accessible to all people, regardless of religious affiliation. As Westerners, we may best conceptualize Buddhism as a holistic psychology, as opposed to a religion. And for this reason, for decades, many Western mental health professionals have turned to Buddhism as a means for understanding the human body–mind when devising interventions for supporting various mental health conditions, from anxiety to depression to trauma. As will be discussed, in Buddhism, most everything external is a metaphor for one's own mind—an outer reflection of one's inner landscape.

In reality, there isn't any model of Western psychotherapy that hasn't drawn from Indigenous or Eastern thought. Mindfulness is at the heart of most modern psychotherapies, from cognitive–behavioral therapy, to eye movement desensitization and reprocessing (EMDR), to internal family systems (IFS) therapy, to hakomi, and somatic experiencing (SE). Mindfulness comes from Buddhism. It was a direct teaching of the Buddha.

The primary model of somatic psychotherapy that you'll get to explore in this book comes from the IFS model, which holds both Indigenous and Eastern influence. The practices in this book are somatic and ancestral. When you connect to your body and go inward to practice them, don't be surprised if you are met with a warm familiarity. The wisdom of awakening is in our blood. Returning to this wisdom within our bodies, we find that we've never left home.

HOW TO USE THIS BOOK

The embodiment practices and insights I offer in this text build upon one another. So while the healing journey is far from linear, I do offer that you navigate these pages in the order they are presented. However, there is a caveat—the appendices provide resources to be explored at any time as you make your way through this book. If diaphragmatic breathing, the foundation of all the embodiment practices, is new to you or you could use a refresher, Appendix A provides a tutorial, offering a yogic breath practice called ujjayi pranayama (victorious breath). If you are someone who finds breath work activating as opposed to relaxing, Appendix B offers you alternatives and encouragement. Appendix C is there for you if you're ever feeling a need to temporarily contain or put away an emotional experience for a time.

The embodiment practices in this text are meant to be lifelong resources—they are ones to return to, again and again, and make a part of your regular practice if you choose.

✳

The light in you is what got you here. I am grateful for you and your curiosity, your yearning for more from this life.

Let's again pause and drop in, landing our conscious awareness inside our bodies.

Allow yourself a moment to pause and check in.

What does your body need from you right now?

Movement? Allow yourself to move.

Rest? Is rest something you can embrace right now?

Does your body need you to listen? Can you open your heart and do so?

Breathe slowly. Move gracefully. There is no rush to be anywhere.

The journey itself is the medicine.

May this book be of benefit.

EMBODIED
SELF
AWAKENING

BEYOND SURVIVAL

Bringing Our Pain Onto the Path

Pain is also a vehicle of knowledge.
It might very well be knowledge itself.

—OCEAN VUONG,
"GETTING CLOSE TO THE TERROR WITH OCEAN VUONG"

*T*he seeds of awakening are planted within each one of us. Though we may confuse our pain and the traumas we've survived for our identity, wakefulness is our natural state. Before we arrived here, our parents and society at large decided for us who we were supposed to be. But they too, more than likely, misidentified with their pain and were somewhat disconnected from their true nature. Asleep to the truth within and around them, the narratives they projected onto us were also false. Yet, on some level, we believed them. And now, we're still carrying the baggage.

Not only in childhood, but as adults, we've survived quite a lot. Regardless of our personal trauma history, simply living in a society where the collective burdens of white body supremacy, the cis-hetero-patriarchy, and capitalism continue to violate the humanity of so many, we are all harmed in our own way.[1] It can become so painful inside that it's far easier to focus outward, and we become more and more distanced from our truth over time. But there is hope for us.

Pain and trauma do not halt our personal evolution or spiritual progression. They provide us an opportunity to wake up all the more. This involves doing something different, amid the cultural norms of repressing what feels unbearable and inevitably taking out our pain on others. Instead, bringing our pain onto the path, we make a conscious effort to be with our pain in a compassionate way in which we not only heal it but evolve from it.

When we push the unpleasant down and out of our awareness, we are making a choice not to see—to turn a blind eye to the suffering happening directly inside of us. When we turn away from the pain inside, we then replicate this pattern with the pain happening around us—we block it out.

We put a veil of protection over our eyes, choosing not to look at the reality of our world, within and outside ourselves. This form of denial is cultural and has contributed to the collective trauma that pervades our society.

There is another option—the one offered in this book. It is an option infused with radical compassion, where we turn toward what hurts deep within. This option lends itself to spaciousness, peace within, deep healing, and, in the end, freedom.

The thought of being with pain, memory, and leftover trauma stored in the body can feel scary or overwhelming, but there is a way to do this that is compassionate and that works with the pace of each unique nervous system. Lifting the veil happens gradually, over time. Awakening, the process of seeing clearly again, of returning to our true nature, is skillful and sacred—not to be rushed. It's liberative.

The first step along our path of awakening involves becoming embodied. Without embodiment, we lose our connection to the present moment, and we can't then do the spiritual work to awaken. Embodiment arrives with a conscious connection to the body, joined by the capacity to effectively regulate our nervous system and stay present with the body regardless of whether what we experience in the body is pleasurable, painful, or something else altogether. We maintain the ability to stay with the experience in the body without going into a trauma response such as fight, flight, freeze, or shutdown.

As trauma survivors, the obstacle here is that trauma takes us out of the body, resulting in disembodiment.

*

TRAUMA AND DISEMBODIMENT

We'll expand on the definition of "trauma" as we continue along this journey together, but for now, trauma can be understood in two dimensions. First, trauma can be that which is too much, too fast, too soon—meaning our nervous systems are unable to cope with the stimuli being thrown their way.[2] Second, trauma can be described as too little for too long—meaning our basic human and spiritual needs are not being met by our environment. In response, our nervous systems begin to quiet and shut down for our own survival.

During trauma, our bodies are active, our nervous systems running the show in their best attempts to ensure our survival; however, we tend to be disconnected from our bodies and what is happening inside because experiences of trauma overwhelm our ability to stay embodied and present. Embodiment, on the other hand, is safety inside. With embodiment, we recognize our bodies, our hearts, as home.

Embodiment is a grounded and calm sense of ease that allows us the capacity to open our hearts and pour compassion inward and outward. But trauma creates a barrier here. Trauma lends itself to disembodiment. Trauma propels our bodies into survival mode. We may experience a nervous system state of upregulation (fight, flight, or active freeze). With the blood rushing to our arms and legs, we may be compelled to literally fight or run, and if we are unable to do so successfully, our bodies may freeze while all the chemicals and adrenaline of fight or flight continue to percolate inside.

In the long term, we may be hypervigilant with fear of a looming threat or danger, anxious with racing thoughts, or may experience physical sensations that present a sense of dis-ease in the body. Rather than upregulation, what we experience may be a nervous system state of downregulation (freeze with collapse)—one where we are hypovigilant, shut down, numb, distanced, detached, emotionally collapsed, or immobilized. While our bodies take us into these extreme nervous system states in their attempt to keep us alive, it is not safe, nor is life as satisfying when we are stuck in one of these extreme states long-term.

It is natural that we will experience moments of dysregulation on any given day, because life brings the unexpected or unpleasant our way, and that's okay. However, being in one of these extreme states long-term leads to disembodiment. Disembodiment is disconnection, and disconnection leads to dissatisfaction. Disconnected from the world within and around us, we get a sense that something is missing from this life—a spiritual crisis of some kind results.

Talia (she/her) was a survivor of childhood sexual abuse (CSA). To survive the decades of horror that colored her past, parts of Talia had removed her awareness from her body to keep her safe—to make the abuse she endured less painful and the knowing that it would happen again less real. The survival strategy Talia's body chose protected her in childhood. While it didn't prevent the abuse from occurring, it distanced her slightly from the reality of it.

Now an adult, Talia entered therapy because she desperately wanted love and a lifelong partner, but she was struggling to exist from day to day. As our nervous system has no concept of time, Talia's body responded to daily interactions as though the abuse of her childhood was still looming around the corner. A glance from a stranger in the grocery store could send her body into an upregulated state of fight or flight, and she feared for her safety and life.

When attempting to be intimate with a romantic interest, her body would send her into a downregulated state of freeze with collapse. She would dissociate, check out, and leave her body, and this would, in her words, "freak out" her romantic interests. They would leave, never to talk to her again. Memories of abandonment from her childhood, stored in her body, often rushed to the surface. Talia was often left feeling numb, depressed, alone, and unlovable. Hopelessness

*and purposelessness marked Talia's daily experience. Talia
described feeling disconnected from life—like an observer
rather than a participant.*

HEALING TRAUMA AND RETURNING HOME

The body is the vehicle that lands our soul here in this earthly realm.
Through our body we experience our humanity. Through our body we
access our capacity for awakening. Healing trauma and the wounds of
our past is both a spiritual endeavor and one in which the body, and our
connection to it, is vital. Home is in the body.

Disembodiment is a disconnect from our body–home. With it, we
struggle to feel comfortable in our own skin—the intuitive wisdom
within, the internal resources, and the connection to our true nature
seem out of reach. Disembodiment is the direct consequence of trauma.
Whether we have survived abuse, like Talia, or not, we've survived
something—something we may not even recognize as trauma but which
our body holds onto as such. As a result, many of us are somewhat disconnected from our bodies.

This is exacerbated in a success-driven society that privileges
endeavors of the mind over those of the heart—a capitalist society that
ties our worth to our productivity, output, and economic success. We're
conditioned to push away our pain or take a pill to mask it, so that we
can continue to produce and make it in such a fast-paced culture. Not
to mention, the cultural legacy burdens of white body supremacy and
the cis-hetero-patriarchy have us all feeling at least a little fragmented
inside, since we know deep within that the messages these systems
reinforce are false, violent, and manipulative.

On a nervous system level, disembodiment leads to glitches that injure our nervous system's ability to effectively detect threat and safety alike. We may have difficulties relating to others socially, as our body is more focused on survival. We may perceive threat constantly, be terrified by intimate connections with others, and struggle to ever feel a sense of being at home in the body.

Dissociation is one form of disembodiment—a trauma response where the mind leaves the body in an attempt to keep us alive and to survive the pain of the trauma we're experiencing. When we dissociate, we are no longer connected to our bodies in the present moment. It's not uncommon for survivors of childhood sexual abuse, as they recount the abuse in adulthood, to describe having felt that they were floating up above themselves looking down at the abuse happening, as though they were outside their bodies. For their survival, their nervous systems took them out.

Many childhood abuse survivors, like Talia, continue to experience episodes of dissociation into adulthood. Trauma, stored as implicit memory in the body, has no sense of time.[3] During the abuse, dissociation saved Talia by distancing her from the reality that was the torture of the assaults. However, as an adult, Talia's nervous system continued to respond as though the abuse was still happening. Survivors like Talia, who continue to experience dissociative episodes into adulthood, often experience a generalized level of disembodiment, meaning that there is a disconnect from one's body and its cues most of the time, even when not in a full dissociative episode. This can all change, however, with healing and practices that intentionally increase embodiment, such as the ones offered in this book.

As you can imagine, to experience generalized disembodiment or dissociative episodes long term is far from ideal. While the pain of life may be minimally distanced, we are also distanced from the joy. However, dissociation and disembodiment do not have to be seen as pathologies. Anything that could be viewed as a pathology can be reframed through a compassionate lens and understood with greater accuracy.

My lens is that dissociation is a creative survival response our body may automatically go into when what we are enduring in the present is too overwhelming for our nervous system to effectively cope with. Disembodiment in general is a protective reaction from our nervous system. For many abuse and assault survivors, being present with the body would flood them and send them into a trauma response in which the body feels like it's reliving the trauma all over again, as implicit memories of the abuse are stored in the body. So if you have trouble staying present with your body, be compassionate toward yourself if you can. In time, with intention, things will shift for you.

We are all abuse survivors of some kind. Many of us abuse ourselves, turning away from the wounds within that so greatly need our love and care. Why do we do this? Our nervous systems are driven by a dire need to avoid being overwhelmed. For many of us, the painful emotions hijack our system. We can't stay present with them. We lose control of our body–mind.[4] We're flooded with fear, or we attack the person closest to us, saying things we later regret. We dissociate or black out, or we choose to take ourselves out, escaping our body with drugs, alcohol, food, sex, or behaviors that numb, distract, and distance us from ourselves.

There's a better way. Pushing our pain down or running from it further imprisons us. Intentionally locating our pain and choosing to bring it onto our healing path is liberative. Attending to our pain with compassion, working with our trauma somatically, we heal and become more embodied. As we heal, we wake up. We begin to notice what we couldn't see before.

Through this process, the injustices we once carried in our bodies, hearts, and minds are illuminated. We go to those dark corners within, with compassion, and offer them healing. We begin to see clearly again. *Practice in being with our own shadows equips us to investigate the shadows of the world.* And we can now do this while remaining embodied— we can extend the compassion of our hearts outward and recognize that the violence we see outside ourselves is nothing more than beings entrenched in their own deep suffering.

SEPARATION FROM OUR BODIES LEADS TO SEPARATION FROM ONE ANOTHER

Growing up in a colonized society with a dark, shadowed past, many of us know ourselves as little as we know our true, collective history. Within our Western education system, in-depth, unbiased coverage of the horrors of the transatlantic slave trade and the mass genocide and displacement of the native peoples of the Americas are glossed over if not all together absent.

Our own personal truths, our gifts, our wisdom are also hidden by the biases conditioned into us. We are not seeing things clearly. We are offered privilege in some areas, and in others we are oppressed, and from this, our biases dance around inside us and inform every relationship we have, including the one we have with ourselves.

We house our biases in our bodies. Our bodies often no longer feel like home, but rather a foreign, intimidating, unknown land. In turn, we colonize ourselves, abandoning parts of ourselves that we've come to believe are bad, frightening, or unbearable. Rather than offer these parts of ourselves time and compassion, we attempt to will them to change or force new ways of being onto them.

The paths of spiritual evolution and decolonization are one. Decolonization is the practice of repairing the impacts of disembodiment, which are a direct result of separation. It's a path of creating intentional repair between body, mind, heart, and spirit, from the harmful disembodiment that is a direct consequence of colonialism.

We have become very good at learning—at digesting and internalizing the beliefs of others. Decolonizing involves thinking for ourselves, questioning what we have learned with discernment, examining what we think we know, exploring our conditioning, listening inward and outward, healing with intention, opening our hearts, and returning to our true nature—that which is not separateness and hate, but union and love.

We are on unceded land. And most of us are here because of enslavement, colonialism, or some other form of violence perpetrated by or against our ancestors. Where goes violence, so too goes disembodiment. Disembodiment is a trauma response. And colonialism and disembodiment are both a disconnection of mind from body, of head from heart.

Just as it is through the body that we connect to our humanity, with disembodiment we are disconnected from our own humanness. Disconnected in this way, we dehumanize ourselves, and what follows is that we project this outward and dehumanize others. Disconnected from our hearts and our humanity, never having touched our own shadows, we inflict pain, harm, and injury outward.

When disconnected people, suffering from the injury of separateness, obtain wealth and power, the amount of pain they inflict is devastating. Beings who are suffering create more suffering.

Separation is the natural consequence of trauma. Trauma creates a fragmentation inside. Memories are fragmented. Our minds and bodies don't communicate as they did before. We experience inner polarizations—parts of us feel guilt and shame, are outraged, or even blame ourselves for what we've survived, and other parts of us are numb, hopeless, or helpless.

When we feel separate inside, our minds distanced from our hearts, we live in that separateness, and we create separateness all around us.

Some of us struggle with depression. We may feel defective, alone, like we don't belong, that we don't matter. The separateness we sense between ourselves and others heightens the suffering deep within.

Clinging to this sense of separateness halts our liberation. The gift of this precious human life is that it provides an opportunity for our awakening, and it does this while allowing us to be a part of something much larger than ourselves. Our willingness to include is an act of compassion—our willingness to include the parts of ourselves that we tend to run from, and our willingness to include the parts of others for which we feel contempt. We must examine what it is that keeps us from extending compassion inward and outward and offer these sacred parts of ourselves the healing they've long been awaiting.

LESSONS OF AWAKENING

More than 2,500 years ago, around 563 BC, in the town of Lumbini, at the southern end of Nepal where it borders northeastern India, lived a man named Siddhartha Gautama. He would come to be known as the Buddha. "Buddha" is a Pali word that literally translates as "awakened." His Holiness the Dalai Lama describes the Buddha as a "symbol of peace, symbol of compassion, symbol of nonviolence," a representation of "our own potential to know the ultimate reality."[5]

Buddhism is a holistic psychology. It's a system for compassionately examining the causes and conditions for our suffering while offering effective ways to alleviate our suffering and live a life where we experience joy and freedom. It's a method for awakening and connecting to the wisdom within through the practices of meditation and contemplation.

Buddhism is also a decolonization practice. As Pamela Ayo Yetunde and Cheryl A. Giles describe in their anthology *Black and Buddhist*,

"Buddhism is a path to de-caste or decolonize one's mind while simultaneously helping oneself build resilience against trauma."[6] The dharma, the teachings of the Buddha, support us in healing trauma and retraining the body–mind to see what is really in front of us, as opposed to that which is the appearance of our own trauma reflected back at us.

The Buddha was a person of culture who at a young age recognized injustice, and whose journey to awakening commenced with his rejection of the oppressive caste system in South Asia at the time—a system that reinforced attitudes of separateness and dynamics of privilege and oppression.[7] Born into nobility, the Buddha renounced his wealth and privilege, understanding that they wouldn't bring him lasting happiness, nor would they protect him from the trauma, decay, and eventually death that come as a result of living this life and having a body.

He was determined to touch something deeper, some greater aspect of truth that might liberate him, and possibly others, from the suffering and polarization created within his own body–mind. The night of his awakening, sitting in deep meditation under the Bodhi tree, the Buddha was met with his own inner fragmentation. Pain, self-doubt, and restlessness arose from within him. Determined, not turning away from this pain but witnessing it, even befriending it, he eventually attained enlightenment that evening under the light of the full moon.

Much of Buddhism, as we'll explore together, is ultimately about befriending our own inner afflictions, recognizing that the appearance of an enemy or an ally is the making of our own mind. In reality, there is a nondual nature to all that exists. Coming to this experience in an embodied way, the Buddha awakened. Following his awakening, the Buddha thought long and hard about teaching. He thought perhaps his teachings were too "against the stream." Having rejected the oppressive caste system and having expanded his awareness to some truths that opposed the dominant belief structure of the time, he knew he might be up for pushback.

But the Buddha chose to remain active in the world—awake in the world. He could have remained a recluse in the woods, peaceful and liberated from the suffering of the world. But instead, he chose the world. He chose the sentient beings who had not yet achieved awakening. This is what nobility really looks like. It is this concept, "no being left behind"—a wisdom-rich, embodied understanding that in reality none of us are truly free until all of us are free.

The Buddha chose to return and teach a small group of monks what he had recognized the night of his awakening. The Buddha's teachings, now formalized into a tradition we know as Buddhism, offer us tools to go inward and connect to the true nature of reality and, in turn, to alleviate our suffering. This embodied understanding of the nature of reality is both our liberation and our awakening. It clears any notion of separateness we have internalized and frees us to experience the non-dual, luminous ground of being.

We cannot awaken as long as we are holding separateness or prejudice in our bodies, hearts, and minds. Yet when we attend to, care for, and heal that within us which creates separation, the seeds of awakening already planted within us are inspired to grow. Self-awakening is the conscious, ongoing process of liberating ourselves from the overriding sense of duality or separateness that has characterized so much of our brief existence. It's loosening our grasp on these ideas of "me" and "mine," opening our minds to new ideas that may be uncomfortable, but will surely expand our consciousness.

LIFE BRINGS TRAUMA

One of the Buddha's first teachings, which stands at the core of Buddhism outside of school or tradition, was the Four Noble Truths.[8] The first of the Four Noble Truths is "life brings dukkha." "Dukkha" is a Pali word that translates as "unsatisfactoriness," though it is commonly translated as "suffering." Life brings suffering. In other words, life brings trauma.

Ultimately, suffering has to do with need and desire—it comes down to not getting what we needed, wanted, or hoped for. Remember, trauma is both that which is too much, too fast, too soon, or too little for too long. In childhood we had foundational needs that were critical to our development of a healthy sense of self. When these core human needs remain unmet in childhood, it's then common as adults to project outward the sense of lack we feel inside. We crave and desire the material: wealth, power, control, possessions (which include other people), thinking that if we get this or that, the unsatisfactoriness of life will melt away. "*Then* I'll be happy," we think.

We suffer because we get stuck—we get wrapped in the narratives around our experiences with life: "He did this to me." "I must be unlovable. Why is it so hard to love me?" "This pain is who I am now. I'm broken." "I'm going to get them back for this. Fuck that!" We suffer because our bodies hold onto the experience, and we reexperience an outdated situation over and over again—our nervous systems without concept of time or opportunity to release the pain.

This human life makes us vulnerable to suffering. Our capacity to love deeply and heal deeply accompanies our capacity to fear deeply, to weep deeply, and to be deeply heartbroken by what is happening in our world. We are sensitive to all of it. And it's this sensitivity that is our potential for wakefulness. Culturally, we think sensitivity is a weakness, but what if it's moreso an alertness that allows us to be awake and attuned to what's happening in the world?

Life includes suffering. Parts of us may protest upon hearing this. This is what we fight against. We want life to be all pleasure and no pain. "All" is not part of the equation of life. There is no light without darkness. Frankie Beverly was onto something when he said, "Joy and pain are like sunshine and rain."[9] Do you remember the lyrics?

Well, Frankie and the Buddha were teaching the same thing, y'all. Pleasure and pain are different sides of the same coin. Could one even exist without the other?

To reflect, the Buddha didn't teach that life is *all* suffering. There is joy, and love, and even freedom can be a part of this life. But our human tendency is to work hard to escape what we fear will be uncomfortable. Ironically, discomfort is a gateway to awakening. We want to experience only what is love and light, and we mistakenly think that we must be doing something wrong when this is not the case. We think we need to try harder at life and continue to pursue all the remedies outside of us when the real antidote is within.

Life is not all suffering, but suffering is a part of life. That's the first noble truth. The second truth? There is a cause to our suffering. Suffering's root cause is our own injury of separateness, carried by none other than the ego. And what's the third truth? There is a way out of suffering. The fourth? The way out of suffering is the path of awakening itself.

HEALING THE EGO'S SENSE OF SEPARATENESS

There is a way to suffer less, and it involves healing and releasing the grip of our own tightly bound egoic self. In the West, when we hear the word "ego," we may automatically think of an annoying arrogance that plagues many others, but not us, of course. Particularly if we suffer from low self-worth or esteem, incredibly common in this culture, we may think we don't have an ego issue. While arrogance is one way in which the ego manifests, it's more encompassing than that. In Eastern culture and tradition, where this term derives, the ego is the part(s) of us that sees the world through the lens of "I," "me," "mine."[10]

We all have an ego, whether with an inflated sense of self-esteem or low. Low self-worth is indicative of an ego (sense of self) that never had the opportunity to fully develop. This is common in our society for the reasons mentioned throughout this chapter. The practices in this book will support you in healing and developing a healthy sense of self, or ego, so that eventually its tight grip can loosen and it doesn't have to dominate your life. Life then becomes a lot more joyful.

The ego sees self and "other." Sometimes the ego feels the self is less worthy than others, and sometimes it sees the self as more. Either way, the ego sees separation wherever it goes. It thinks, "I am different," "I'm defective," or "I'm special," "They are not like me," and "This is mine, not theirs." Remember, separation is a natural consequence of trauma. The ego is part of our survival system, and it will run our entire life until we consciously choose to heal our inner situation—attending to the parts of us so desperate for care that they need to distinguish themselves as better or worse than others.

It is the ego that categorizes people and other living beings, creates a hierarchy of them, and both perpetrates and justifies harm toward others. It's the ego that takes ownership of what it believes belongs to it, whether that be pain ("I'm worthless") or gain ("This is my money"), and then clings to that object which it believes it owns—clinging to the pain as "mine," or clinging to the gain as "mine." Yet clinging to something doesn't make it stay, but it does ensure that when it goes, we'll suffer because we were determined to hold on so tightly.

The ego's tendency is toward attachment and grasping. It clings to its own wants, desires, and needs and elevates them above those of others, often unconsciously. Whether with low self-esteem or with flat-out narcissism, the ego interjects itself at the center of existence. The ego's vision is obscured by its own pain, passions, attachments, and aversions.

Ironically, the ego creates separateness but is also triggered by it. The ego experiences gratification when it is the one in the seat of power and control—here separation lends itself to some false feeling of comfort. When we are leading with our ego and we feel a sense of power, we still don't experience a sense of harmony inside, but we're less aware of it.

Yet, when we're not in the seat of power, and therefore we are the one being "othered," the ego can't bear it. It's devastating, and to our nervous system it feels like a threat to our survival, which ultimately, to our nervous system, feels like death.

Can you recall a time you met a stranger that you instantly clicked with? You started having a conversation with this person—maybe you were at the grocery store, maybe at a community meeting, maybe the airport. You started talking to this stranger, and you were both in a pretty good mood, and you learned that you had all these things in common. You each started to share thoughts and ideas and opinions. The energy was vibing, and you were totally present in the satisfying flow of the exchange. Many of us have had exchanges like this.

In that moment of connection, with a complete stranger, we experience something liberative. In that moment, we experience the lack of "other," freedom from separation—our ego suspended. We feel so good afterward because we got a taste of what liberation feels like. It's beautiful that we can experience that in union with another.

Now think about a time when you had a conflict with someone close to you—your child, your significant other(s), your parent, your colleague. When you're in that conflict and you don't feel seen or understood, the energy of separateness is tangible and your ego is highly reactive. Our ego may respond with anger, or rage, or self-loathing, or escape tactics, or usually a number of things. We've been "othered," blamed, misunderstood—our unhealed core wounds from childhood and beyond surface, and our nervous system goes into hyper- or hypo-mobilization.

Exchanges where we don't feel seen or heard, where we feel violated, leave us feeling depleted inside. And oftentimes, in the aftermath of these exchanges, we point the finger outward, instead of looking inward and caring for our pain.

The ego is triggered by the same sense of separateness that it creates. As long as the ego leads in our daily life, we will experience some level of suffering. Integrating a trauma-informed perspective, we can see how the ego is linked to our nervous system and, by way of that, our survival. As the nervous system is always working behind the scenes to determine whether a current situation is safe or poses a threat to our survival, the ego is also very much a threat detector. The ego wants gain and status and detects a threat when its public or personal image is up for question. The ego fights for its survival and fears its own demise.

The ego is ultimately linked to our fear of death. When our nervous system detects a threat, this is what our bodies prepare for. When we go into shutdown mode, also called immobilization, our organ functioning declines, and our bodies literally prepare for death.[11] And it's the ego that will fight to the death to save us when we are faced with a threat to our life, even if this threat is coming by way of a heated argument with our spouse, as opposed to an actual threat to our mortality.

So while it could be easy to vilify the ego, since it is responsible for the majority of our suffering, instead we could pause and consider getting to know this part of ourselves better. How many times has our ego helped save our lives, even if it didn't go about it the best way? To break away from the sense of separation that informs our suffering, we must liberate the ego, but anything that is liberated must first be loved. There will be many opportunities ahead to befriend and heal the many parts of ourselves that make up the ego.

In sum, our pain is not our truth. But with pain comes a powerful opportunity. Because pain is a part of life, we can use it as grounds for dropping into what is real, for reexamining everything, for evolving beyond the claustrophobic confines of how we habitually relate to ourselves and the world. The suffering created by our own repressed ego, the traumas we've survived, the daily annoyances, can all be brought onto the path of healing, which is ultimately the path of awakening.

We cannot awaken if we remain asleep to the pain held within. Any sense of freedom we achieve will be fleeting if we are avoiding the pain imprisoned inside of us. When other people are on our nerves, rather than fixating our awareness outward, we can look within and attend to our deepest core wounds that have been awaiting our care for so very long.

Awakening is our birthright. It's already within us. Pain is a portal to awakening.

EMBODIMENT PRACTICE:
ACKNOWLEDGING THE LAND, LANDING IN THE BODY

Embodiment Preparation

I'd like to invite us to drop in and connect to our bodies. Prior to beginning this practice, I invite us to take several deep breaths as we acknowledge that we are on unceded Indigenous land. That the earth-centered, loving, soulful, native owners of this land were hurt, traumatized, and violently removed from this land, their suffering erased, their descendants alive but often isolated and invisible.

Part of decolonizing our path is working to counteract erasure, so let's pause here and offer a few conscious breaths to honor the native peoples of this land.

If we do not already know of the Indigenous people that originally occupied (and may still occupy) the soil on which we currently stand, I invite you to visit Code for Anchorage's Land Acknowledgement webpage (https://land.codeforanchorage.org/) to help us remember. Upon finding out whose land we're on, I invite us to research these people and offer reverence for their contributions, wisdom, and involuntary sacrifice that have allowed us to live in whatever advantages we experience. I encourage us to consider how we can actively contribute to the uplifting of these people at present, and that we then act—that we contribute and contribute some more, knowing that this life is not about us alone; this life is about all of us together.

Note: If diaphragmatic breathing is new to you, I encourage you to visit Appendix A prior to moving into this embodiment practice. It includes is a tutorial on diaphragmatic breath work with a yogic pranayama (breath practice) called ujjayi pranayama, or victorious breath. Ujjayi is the foundational breath for all of the embodiment practices in this text.

In addition, Appendix B offers support around what to do if deep breathing practices don't soothe your nervous system as they are intended to. Appendix C includes an exercise called containment practice, and it is here for you if any of the embodiment practices in this book bring up anything that is too much, too fast, or too soon.

Please take a moment to find a comfortable space, water, a blanket, a journal, or whatever feels supportive, and join me when you are ready.

✳

EMBODIMENT PRACTICE

I invite you to bring your body to a restful position, and one where you can connect your feet to the earth. You may find that you come to sit in a chair with your feet on the ground, or maybe you find that a standing position feels better for you. Maybe you go outside so that your feet can literally connect to the soil.

Once you find a position for your body that feels somewhat comfortable, I invite you to consciously nourish the connection of your feet against the earth. To do this, imagine that you are standing outside—standing on rich, fertile soil.

Take a moment to press the balls of your feet down into that soil. Press your heels down.

You might try lifting your toes up. Imagine feeling the rich soil move between your toes as you wiggle them around. Notice: What does the soil feel like as you move it between your toes?

Allow your toes to gently relax back into the soil. Let your entire foot, right and left, relax into this rich, fertile earth.

Feel as though your feet are now growing roots down into the soil, that your feet anchor you to the soil and the soil anchors you to this earth.

Take several slow, deep breaths if it feels right.

Feeling the embrace of your feet to the earth, take a moment, several con-

scious breaths, just to acknowledge the land you are on. Acknowledge the land's roots. Acknowledge the ancestors of the land.

Feeling the rootedness of your feet to the earth, take a moment to acknowledge your own ancestors, if this resonates with you.

Feel your connection to all who have walked here before you and who contributed to the healing of the world. Feel that you are supported, by the earth, by the ancestors.

From this deep connection earthward, begin to connect with other parts of your body.

Begin to notice your body.

What do you notice? Is there comfort, ease, expansiveness, or neutrality anywhere inside?

Take several conscious, deep breaths if it feels right.

Is there anything that this comfort, ease, expansiveness, or neutrality is telling you? (E.g., "I am okay," "I am settled.")

Is there a message there, a feeling that arises, a sensation, any information at all?

Continue to breathe deeply, sending your conscious breath like a wave of compassion to the places in your body holding this message, sensation, or information.

Continue this practice for as long as feels right.

✳

When that begins to feel complete, take a couple of clearing breaths. Slowly begin to notice where in your body you feel discomfort, disease, tension, or constriction.

Perhaps it's more of an emotion you notice, like sadness.

Or more of a pervading experience, like grief.

Perhaps it's more of a mood. Whatever you notice is welcome.

What are you noticing?

Can you acknowledge what you notice? Either silently or aloud?

That is, if it's a thought we notice, like "Am I doing this right?", we might acknowledge this question coming from within by saying to it, silently or aloud, "I hear you; you're wondering if we are doing this right."

If it's an ache in our lower back that we notice, we might send the message silently or aloud: "I see you in pain."

Stay with any thoughts, emotions, or physical sensations you experience.

As you focus on them, what do you notice? Do any new thoughts, emotions, or physical sensations arise?

Can you offer curiosity, compassion, or gratitude toward what you are noticing?

Continue to focus on that experience if it feels right. Be with it and breathe with it.

Continue to offer gratitude, compassion, curiosity, whatever feels right. If none of that is available, that is okay too. There is no incorrect experience to have. It's all welcome.

In whatever way feels right, let your body know that while this practice is closing, you will return later in time. Offer gratitude to your body, if possible, for informing you of its experience.

✳

Breathing consciously, bring your attention back to your feet against the soil.

What do you notice now?

Send gratitude to the land for holding you up, for carrying you.

Send gratitude to the ancestors and your roots, if it feels right.

Take a moment to honor your efforts and anything that showed up for you during this practice. Take a moment to honor, again, your connection to the earth and your roots.

When it feels right, open your eyes and take your time to journal, record, and/or reflect before moving onward.

CLOSING WITH INTENTION

I invite you to continue to stay present with your body as you move through your day. Notice the physical (somatic) sensations; the emotions and feeling states; your energy level; your thoughts, ideas, and attitudes—inviting increased presence moment by moment.

Tune into how you respond to your emotional, mental, and physical pain, both when by yourself and when interacting with other people. What is your relationship to pain, and how do you respond to it in yourself? How do you respond when people you love are in pain? Neutral people? Strangers? No need to judge. The path of awakening begins with increased awareness, without getting entangled in some narrative of judgment.

Where inside are you holding a sense of separation? Are there parts of you, emotions, or ways of being within you that you like and elevate above others? Parts of you, emotions, or ways of being that you dislike, avoid, or hide from others?

I invite you to be gentle with yourself throughout this self-inquiry. Stay curious about your relationship to pain. Again, our tendency is to fight it, but when we soften our hearts to it, we find that pain is actually a portal to awakening.

May the healing and benefits obtained by way of these words contribute to the liberation of all beings, living and nonliving, without exception.

2

THE ESSENCE OF EMPTINESS

Living beings are as limitless as space itself.

—DILGO KHYENTSE,
THE HEART OF COMPASSION[1]

*I*n *Chapter One, we left off* speaking to the ego, the aspect of our-selves that sees the world through the lens of "I," "me," and "mine." This is the part of us that divides the world into self and other. Yet, as much as the ego creates separateness, it is also negatively activated by it.[2] Putting itself at the center of all situations, its threat detector is hyperactive—it fears it's constantly up for attack and perceives attack at times when it's not really there.

The ego is always working under the radar, oftentimes outside of our conscious awareness, both to prevent assaults and to fight back against them should they occur. Working to prevent character assaults can look like people pleasing, perfectionism, avoidance, and the like, while pre-paring to fight against attacks can look like imagining scenarios of future assaults in our mind and practicing in our heads how we would respond to defend ourselves. Sometimes it even looks like unconsciously put-ting ourselves in situations similar to the ones in which we experienced trauma, to attempt a "do-over" and gain mastery over the situation.

The ego clings most tightly to its own identity, made up of the body-mind-consciousness, and works to maintain or elevate itself in reputation, wealth, power, status, influence, and so on. When the ego takes leader-ship in our life, the wisdom of our awakening, compassionate hearts is obscured by the ego's fixations. Invested in self-interest, the ego must take a back seat for the light of authentic compassion to shine through.

Before we go further, I invite us to pause and remember that while it's not difficult to criminalize the ego, given our cultural tendency to see things in the form of binaries—good or bad, wrong or right—there's no good in denigrating this part of ourselves. As survivors of trauma, as we all are, our ego has saved us many times. How many times have we offered it gratitude? How many times have we consciously connected to it in our bodies and listened to what it has to say? If your answer is "none," that's okay. That's what this book is here for.

The path involves getting to know all parts of ourselves with equanimity. If we want to see equality in the world, that journey starts within. All parts are equal—no need to create an inner hierarchy between the parts of ourselves we find most holy and the parts that we disparage most.

The ego means well. Its grasping is linked to its survival. Grasping is our survival instinct. Those who work in hospice witness the immense egoic fear that can arise in people who are unprepared at the time of death. We fight against death. We fight to survive. Our bodies are always attending to our survival. While fighting against any part of ourselves only exacerbates the polarizations we feel inside, befriending our own ego is a powerful healing step not to be skipped on the path.

We cannot transcend the egoic sense of self if we never developed a healthy sense of self to begin with. Talia, whom you met in Chapter One, didn't have her core childhood needs met by the caregivers in her life. Many of us didn't either, whether or not we survived physical or sexual abuse. As children, we need our caregivers to exemplify for us, again and again, that we are unconditionally loved and lovable simply because we are the human beings that we are. We need our caregivers' words and actions to show that there is nothing we must do or say to earn this love—we receive it because we are, and because of that, we belong, we matter, and we are treated with dignity and respect.

We also need attention and care, and to be seen, listened to, and validated. We need a predictable home free from violent outbursts, chronic substance abuse, and dysfunction. If we lose a parent or caregiver, because of death or another form of abandonment, that's a major wound that could interrupt our development. And of course, we need to live in a safe, supportive community, free from violence, and have our basic needs for food, water, clothing, and shelter met.

With all the historical, collective, and systemic trauma that's been passed down and around in this culture, many of us didn't receive all we needed as children, regardless of how stellar our parents were. Over a decade working as a somatic psychotherapist has informed me that perhaps the vast majority of us in this culture are surviving with a fractured sense of self. Western psychology has informed us of the necessity of healthy ego development, while Eastern psychology has clarified for us the necessity of eventually transcending the ego if we are to be happy and free of suffering.

As long as there is unmetabolized trauma in the system, we benefit most by nourishing and healing the ego, neither villainizing it nor spiritually bypassing it. There is no need to rush off toward enlightenment before we've done the work to care for our own shadows. This is really the only way—what is in darkness eventually comes to the light. So let's lay easy on the ego for now. Your inner critic may make it challenging to go easy on yourself. Perhaps you're hearing its voice right now. But the inner critic itself is one aspect of the ego, so you can lay easy on your inner critic too. Show it compassion. Fighting against an inner critic is sure to enliven it all the more.

As we move through the remainder of this chapter, I invite you to remain mindful of your inner dialogue. If you hear that loud critical voice inside, if it begins to berate you, just pause and acknowledge it. You don't have to fight back—that only empowers it to get louder. On the night of his awakening, the Buddha met his own internal critic, he received it with equanimity, and he sent it love. It returned again and again that night as he sat in contemplative meditation, but he kept sending it love, and eventually it transformed. That transformation was essential to the Buddha's awakening.

All parts of us need love, need grace, need a fair chance. Let this be the journey. There is no finish line to rush to. All we need is right here within us, if we're just willing to look. The journey is the medicine.

✳

We spoke about the Buddha's Four Noble Truths. The first truth is, "Life brings suffering (and trauma)." The second noble truth is, "There is a cause to our suffering." This cause is none other than the ego's clinging to what it desires or identifies with. As much as the ego attaches to pleasure, it has an aversion to pain. When I first began studying Buddhism almost two decades ago, it was this teaching that made a huge impact on me: suffering is not pain itself; suffering is an aversion to pain. Our attempts at avoiding pain only exacerbate our suffering. This is the wisdom of bringing pain onto the path—our pain does not have to become our identity. It rather becomes a vehicle for transformation.

The third and fourth noble truths are, "There is a way out of suffering," and "The pathway out is the journey of awakening (and trauma healing) itself." The view within Buddhism is that inherent within each of us is a basic goodness, a tendency toward love and compassion. Even the most violent of individuals have this nature; it's just been obscured by their own trauma and conditioning. These individuals lead with the violent, selfish, or greedy parts of their ego. The light of goodness remains underneath the layers of pain, but with so many layers enveloping it, it becomes hard to access.

Our nature is goodness, and the true nature of our own mind is already awake—already "buddha." This is what we call Buddha Nature, awakened nature. Buddha Nature is inherent in each of us—wisdom, clarity, wakefulness. Trauma cannot destroy it, though it can make it harder to access. Our true nature is an energy of being as opposed to doing. Think how much of a struggle being is for some of us, perhaps particularly for those of us who have survived overt, violent incidents of trauma, or because we live in a society that criminalizes us for being of a particular race, sexual or gender identity, or religious affiliation. Being can be rather complicated. Our nervous systems may maintain a constant state of hyper- or hypo-arousal, and a state of simply being is not so simple at all. Yet our true nature is not obstructed by trauma—it is merely obscured.

When a child falls and scrapes their knee, there's a wound there. But quite naturally, when left alone or attended to with care, the wound heals. The skin that was underneath returns to its original state. Our true nature is like that. It's awake. And though we've been wounded, the healing process naturally follows. As we heal, we return to our natural state. But life keeps hurting us. So we have to get intentional about our healing, intentional about waking up. And if we do, we return closer and closer to the awakened state that is our home.

We are always waking up, but sometimes we fight against the natural process of awakening, clinging to the very ideas, objects, and behaviors that elicit our misery. Though each of our stories is unique, there are similarities too. My journey toward freedom began almost two decades ago. I was in my early twenties and something had to change—I knew the way I was living was not sustainable. There was space there for me to do something different, but for a while I resisted that space. I feared that space. It was marked by the unknown. I filled it up with meaningless transactions that only left me more depleted. But I knew I couldn't keep living like I was living. Because I wasn't really living. It seemed I was working on dying. But the moment that sparked my path of awakening arrived like a flash of light.

A RETURN HOME

Activation warning: In this section I discuss my personal history with an eating disorder. If this may be triggering to you, I invite you to skip to the next section in this chapter, titled The Space, and/or use the embodiment practices within this or the previous chapter to settle your system. There is also the containment practice in Appendix C to support you if your system ever becomes overwhelmed. Thank you for using these practices and for allowing me to share a piece of my story with you.

I was a professional ballet dancer, and incredibly disembodied. It sounds ironic, or even impossible. But it was possible for me. I used my body as the vehicle to make and express art, but I didn't love my body. It was simultaneously my tool for self-expression and my greatest nemesis. To intentionally starve the body—to ignore the body's messages, needs, and cues of hunger long-term—you need to be disconnected. But now, I was ready to connect. An alarm bell had gone off, thanks in part to another dancer in the company. She was the same one who had given me tips on how to ignore hunger cues at the beginning of the season, but on this day, my 21st birthday, it was different.

The day had already been unusual. I had let myself eat a salad earlier. I had gone out for lunch with my brother and sister to celebrate my birthday that afternoon. To eat on the day of a show was not like me. But I was already sensing that 21 needed to create a shift from some dysfunctional norms. The last year had been hell. As I prepared for a show backstage, sitting down in front of a vanity mirror, applying blush over my razor-blade-thin cheekbones, my best friend approached. She walked up behind me. I could see her approaching in my vanity mirror. Her slow waltz over felt exaggerated and dramatic, like she was moving in slow motion. I watched as she bent down, leaned in, and put her mouth to my ear. She whispered, "You look like you're dying." Then she stood up and walked off.

"Well damn!" I was not expecting that. But the girl was always blunt if not incredibly crass. And she was right. I knew it. I had known it for a while. But I just needed somebody who I knew cared about me to say it. I took a long look at myself in the mirror, and the me reflected back was not someone I knew. "You've gone too far, Nityda." This voice from within felt calm and wise. It felt parental. It embraced me. I had been running away from myself. But maybe I was ready to return.

I understood I had been looking outward for the type of unconditional validation that can only come from within. I started eating again. I didn't plan on leaving the ballet company initially, but the studio's walls were lined with floor-to-ceiling mirrors, and my inner critic was too tempted. I decided it was time. I left the career of my dreams and embarked on an intentional healing journey. I decided it was time to start nourishing myself, not just physically but emotionally, spiritually, holistically.

The eating disorder was a symptom of a larger problem, which was layers of unresolved trauma. Trauma that had been passed generationally, trauma that I had lived in childhood, and trauma that I had faced in my adult years as well. Restricting what I ate was my way of self-regulating, managing my anxiety—albeit not very effectively—and distracting myself from the years of traumatic wounding that were buried deep within. I knew the road ahead was long, perhaps never-ending, but I was excited for this journey.

But who was I if not a dancer? While I was uncertain, I sensed my purpose was higher, larger, than what I had previously thought—that there was more that I didn't yet know. And I knew the answers were inside me. I sensed there was something inside that was pristine, wise, radiant. But I couldn't get to it—there was too much anxiety blocking its glow. I had always been drawn toward meditation. In my childhood home, my father had studied yogic philosophy and practiced Buddhism. He was an avid meditator and chanter. He never invited us kids in to meditate with him—that was his time. But I was always drawn toward what he was doing. He seemed transformed when he reemerged from his meditation space.

I decided I would practice yoga and look into Buddhism. I wanted the meditation and the breath work (pranayama) to steady myself, calm my mind, and uncover what was hidden behind the layers of pain and patterning I knew were not me. Witnessing my father and living in Japan for three years as a kid, I had long resonated with Eastern wisdom traditions. I was curious to sit with the philosophical yoga texts and hear what wisdom ancient, wise sages were offering. I was eager to learn what Buddhism was really all about and how I could maybe find some refuge from the anxious preoccupations that seemed to constantly run through my mental space.

I found a yoga class at my university that met three times a week. In the class, we practiced asanas (the physical postures), but we also studied the philosophical texts, and we spent as much time in meditation and practicing pranayama as we did in the physical asana practice. The pranayama was medicine. The deep breathing helped quiet my mind, and I experienced states of consciousness more peaceful than I knew possible.[3] Six months later I unexpectedly found myself in yoga teacher training, and about six months after that I found a Buddhist sangha (community) that met weekly at a yoga studio where I was teaching.

The dharma (the Buddha's teachings) offered me a sense of peace and direction that had been missing in my life. I took refuge in the teachings, and things started to shift. Yoga and meditation became a part of my daily experience. I was devoted to the quiet time on my cushion when I would sit, study, learn, breathe with control, explore my inner landscape, and get more acquainted with what felt really true. My truth, which trauma had removed from my vision, was becoming more and more clear. Every time I opened a yogic or Buddhist text to learn, the text offered me insight and then guided me right back inward to learn more. This resonated so deeply with my soul. I had always sensed that the answers were within.

I sat. I breathed. I inquired. I listened inward. And it wasn't long after, in the spaces between the breath, I found myself. There I was.

I saw myself. I loved myself. Maybe for the first time. The confused, lost, little girl who starved herself until the flesh of her face was papier-mâché thin, I saw her too. In a new light. Really saw her and her suffering. This little girl, so desperately needing love and care, was a part of me, and I could help her heal. And I did. I turned toward her. I loved her up. She had been waiting for me for so long.

I gave her all the love, in all the ways she needed. My ability to love matched her needs perfectly. When she felt loved by me, she healed, and together we went in and gathered the other little ones inside who had long been waiting and helped them heal too. And we danced and sang and created a beautiful ritual, all in a circle, this mandala (circle) of freedom that I envisioned in my mind and experienced in my body. The ancestors were there too—lifting us up, rooting for us. We all helped each other heal. Together we were free.

The healing journey is never ending. I am still on it. I will always be. It is wild, and messy; scary at times, ecstatic at others. I cannot imagine my life without this journey. Without it, you surely would not be holding this book. Thank you for attending to a piece of my journey. I truly believe in yours.

THE SPACE

Buddhism is a holistic, somatic psychology in which we investigate, and come to experience, the true nature of mind. As the mind's projections create the world we see, through understanding the true nature of mind, we understand the ultimate nature of reality. Our true nature is that of a Buddha, an awakened one. However, to read this as a concept, even to have an enlightened master teacher explain it to us, doesn't allow for its realization. Awakening is a personal experience. The true nature of mind is what we experience as we awaken. As an experience, the true nature of mind is beyond conceptualization—it is not an object to be observed. It's a ground of being, and meditation is the vehicle for attainment of this embodied wisdom.

Yet and still, before going into meditation to experience our true nature, we need some type of guidance around what to look for—after all, when we go inside, we are met with so much that is not (our afflictions). In an attempt to give some pointing-out instruction to his disciples, the Buddha used the word "shunyata," or "emptiness," to describe the nature of mind. As Westerners, we associate the word "emptiness" with the negative. When a client comes in looking depressed and says they feel empty inside, they are speaking to a feeling of lack, an inadequacy, or a void. Yet, the "emptiness" we refer to in Buddhism is quite different from the emptiness we describe in Western dialect.

This emptiness is an expansive field of being where anything and everything is possible, including our healing, including our return home, including our awakening. Yet, to understand emptiness in this way is challenging for several reasons. One, as Westerners, it will take time for us to associate emptiness with something positive and liberative as opposed to something negative and limiting. And two, as the Buddha explained himself, this state is truly indescribable in words. As Khenchen Thrangu teaches in his sacred discourse, *Pointing Out the Dharmakaya,* the nature of mind "can be recognized but not pinpointed like an echo in space."[4]

This vast field is beyond the notions of conceptualization, beyond the notions of duality (the observer and what is being observed). So how can we explain it to those seeking to experience it within? We can't pinpoint it because, as my teacher Lopön Charlotte Rotterdam expresses, "If that's it, then what's over there?"[5] Something separate. But this space is free from separation—free from duality. We can't truly express it in words, so to get as close as possible, we use a simile—we say that the true nature of mind is empty, like space.

Think about what space is. How would you describe space? Think about how we need space and are irritated or exhausted when we don't get it. How many times have you found yourself saying or thinking, "I need my space"? We set boundaries with people when they don't give us the space we desire. We need space because it's our nature. Space is freedom.

Think about how, with space in our schedules, we can relax and rejuvenate ourselves—with space in our minds we can create, we can take a breath, we can think more clearly, or think less if that's what's desired. Space allows for everything—all things arise out of space. Think about how trauma takes up space inside. We can't focus on the things we used to focus on when our bodies are hijacked by fight, flight, or freeze activity. When we are overwhelmed by fear, there is less space to live and to love.

So emptiness is like space. This is a key aspect of our nature. And as Lopön Charlotte explains, this space is not neutral space. It's generative. It's able to produce. Space allows for all things to arise, exist, and cease. This spaciousness that is our nature is free from ego-clinging. It's free from mental fabrication (thoughts, opinions, biases, and fears). It's free from desire, free from aversion, free from affliction and obstacles. This space is freedom itself. It allows for everything. It does not attach to or avert from anything. So it's a space characterized by equanimity or equality. This spaciousness, free of subject and object, knower and what is known, is truly nondual. The ego, who sees separateness, is self-liberated here.

We learn how to experience this spacious nature of ours in deep meditation. Yet, to attain this state you cannot grasp at it like it's some object to obtain. And to remain in this spaciousness in meditation, you cannot cling to it to try and make it stay. If you try to will its arrival, you won't get there, because this is a ground of being, not a ground of doing. If you experience a glimmer of it and try to make it stay, it will surely dissipate. Spaciousness means there's nothing to grasp. It's ungraspable. If you take a moment now to look at the space in front of you, can you reach out and grasp it? No, because you can't grasp air. Air cannot be contained. Our true nature is like that. Boundless. Its potential is limitless. We may limit ourselves, but our nature is free from limitations.

This space exists as a ground of being, meaning it exists as it is organically—it doesn't have to make effort in order to be. As Lopön Charlotte explains, "Space does not effort to hold what it holds." Landing and staying in the ground of true being involves releasing effort. It involves resting in our true nature. This takes practice and patience, as the ego struggles to release its efforts. By befriending the ego, as we'll be doing together in the pages to come, and giving it what it needs, its grip softens, and we get closer and closer to the ground of equanimity—the allowance for everything and the aversion to nothing.

This wisdom of emptiness is an experience we'll be working with in our next embodiment practice. As an idea, we can't fully grasp it intellectually, because again, spaciousness means there is nothing to grasp.

So the nature of mind is emptiness, emptiness being truly beyond description but similar to space. And it's more than that. The sacred texts within the Tibetan Buddhist tradition describe emptiness as space united with awareness. Awareness is an expansive form of presence. As vast as space is, awareness is also like that. Awareness is a receiving of all phenomena that arise and cease within the space. Space and awareness energize one another. They need one another to exist. This is the "emptiness" we refer to in Buddhism. It's not a void or lack; it's space and awareness. Jérôme Edou, in *Machig Labdrön and the Foundations of Chöd*, describes emptiness as "the naturally open and serene state of mind."[6]

Again, it may be hard to wrap your head around this. It took me reading many texts and studying with multiple teachers and, most of all, coming to my own understanding through regular meditation practice. But I include this here so you can explore it in the meditation practices to come—you can see how it lands in your system. And even a conceptual understanding of emptiness can support us as we approach the practices of befriending the ego and the various parts of us that keep us from feeling free.

Emptiness is our true nature—it's like space and awareness united. And there's one more piece—one more attribute used to describe this indescribable ground of being that is the nature of mind.

The term often used is "luminosity," sometimes referred to as "clarity," or "radiance," or "cognitive lucidity." This luminosity is an awakeness. It's the spark that adds life and vividness to the emptiness. As Francesca Fremantle writes, "Inseparable from emptiness is the luminosity—the presence of what is real, the basic ground in which the play of life takes place."[7] This luminosity is wisdom; it's cognizant; it is capable of knowing itself. As Khenchen Thrangu explains, "The mind, being awareness, can experience its own awareness."[8]

So the true nature of mind is emptiness (space and awareness) plus luminosity (the light of wisdom—the mind's ability to know itself). And this is our Buddha Nature—our natural state of wakefulness is this empty, luminous state. The mind is quiet, open, aware, and wise. And its spaciousness is a ground of equanimity—equanimity is a state of having neither an attachment to nor an aversion toward anything. It is a space free of clinging to and also free of pushing away. It's a space that allows for everything, can birth anything, can hold all things without effort. Equanimity means there is no discrimination about what arises. There is no sense of separateness or pain here. The nature of mind is something we can experience in meditation, when we can become and remain embodied, and when our mind gets quiet enough to experience its own subtle yet profound nature.

᛭

This idea of spaciousness is found cross-culturally within the Indig-enous wisdom traditions. I am grateful for the work of my teacher Malidoma Patrice Somé, which has connected me to the wisdom of my ancestors. Somé grew up in an Indigenous Afrikan village, a member of the Dagara tribe of Burkina Faso, in West Afrika. In his text *The Heal-ing Wisdom of Africa*, Somé speaks not only to the spaciousness that is our nature but to the preciousness of taking human form, a practice common to Tibetans:

> The indigenous belief of the Dagara is that we are primarily Spirit. In order to exist as material beings, we have to take a form, and there is the sense among my people that to be in mat-ter is not the most familiar or suitable form for us. To fit ourselves into the narrow part of the universe that allows energy to exist as matter takes some getting used to, and we only bother with it at all because it serves the useful and unavoidable purpose of expanding the spirit in us. It's as if in order to expand or to grow, one must contract and squeeze. The contracted form of our vol-atile spirit in this body. The adventures of the body prepare the spirit for the leap into its next phase of growth.[9]

What Somé is expressing, in a slightly different way, is that the spirit being and the world of spirit itself is like space. To come into human form, we must contract to fit "the narrow part of the universe that allows energy to exist as matter." We must take something boundless, us as we exist in our true nature, and contract it to fit into something defined by boundary—a human body. If our true nature is boundless, beyond the confines of a form, why bother? Because this human life is a precious gift. Having a body brings its challenges. With a body we are susceptible to pain, trauma, and suffering. Yet having a body also brings a unique opportunity where we can experience that pain and use it to evolve spiritually should we get intentional about bringing our pain onto the path along this human journey. I resonate with his words, "the adventures of the body." That is what this life is, an adventure. Especially if we can allow for pain and pleasure alike and invite it all to be a part of this ongoing escapade.

WHAT ABOUT ME?

A lot of clients come to me feeling lost as to who they are. Like most of us, they are trying to be somebody—that's what we're taught. That's likely what our parents wanted for us. And it's definitely what society emphasizes. We're supposed to grow up and "be somebody"—"somebody" meaning successful, with some level of power and wealth, and with a steady career. It's all related to the material. Moreover, this idea of "being somebody" implies that the "somebody" is a solid and fixed persona—"Oh yeah, you know Ashanti, she's x, y, and z." It's comfortable for us when Ashanti is x, y, and z. Then we can recognize her—and her predictability brings us a sense of ease. She fits nicely into the box our ego ascribes her to. But what if Ashanti is not this contracted, fixed being? What if she's dynamic and always changing and because of that you can't really grasp at what or who she is, because her true nature is far more expansive than that?

Many of us are trying to construct something solid. We're trying to build ourselves up and build up our lives to achieve this and gain that, and then we can be "somebody," and then we'll be happy. All we really want is to be loved and to be happy. But what we build and what we construct is never enough—we always want more. Again, if we didn't have safe grounds to develop a healthy sense of ego identity as a child, as adults we constantly crave and seek that development of self.

In a material-driven society, we focus on gain and seek to build something up, because no one ever helped us understand how freedom really works. True freedom comes from accumulating nothing. It comes rather from letting go of everything—releasing the conditioning we've internalized that makes us feel as though we're not enough as we are. When we let go of the faulty beliefs we've ascribed to ourselves, we are boundless. But letting go cannot be forced. And it doesn't happen overnight. It comes in time with healing and awakening. And letting go is scary. Many of us would sooner overidentify with our suffering than release it and fall into the space of the unknown.

> *Arin (they/them) spent a lot of time engulfed in what they described as a "sea of sadness." So much of Arin wanted to feel better, to evolve beyond their childhood trauma and abandonment by their father. Yet there was a polarization inside. When working with the part of Arin that held the sadness, another more protective part would jump in and disrupt the work, making it harder to access the sadness in Arin's body. When engaging with this protective part of themselves, Arin asked the part what it feared would happen if they worked with this sadness, and Arin sensed the part's response: "If I don't have this sadness, who will I be?" Arin had been depressed for a long time, to the point where parts of them thought sadness was just who they were. These parts feared Arin's liberation—they had come to identify with the very thing that kept them from feeling free.*

⁕

The Buddha taught that all phenomena are empty, including self. So not only is the true nature of mind empty, and the true nature of reality empty, but self is also empty. Self is space and awareness—empty. Empty implies equality. If all things are empty, all things are equal. If self is empty, then it's equal with all other aspects of existence. Self doesn't like that. The ego's survival mechanism is to project either its superiority or inferiority compared to others—either way, whether superior or inferior, its difference allows for some level of significance. Even if I have low self-esteem and I believe I am less than you, that still gives me some form of significance, because now "I am different," or "I am defective," and that makes me stand out in some way.

Self is empty. Empty here means empty of solidity. Empty of independent origin. To elaborate on this, the Buddha taught two other important concepts—dependent origination and impermanence. Dependent origination means that nothing exists independently in and of itself without the causes and conditions that contribute to its origin. Take your kitchen table. How did it get here? Someone had an idea to build it. Their idea came from their initial understanding of what a table is and its function, which came from being conditioned into their particular culture and the consequent cultural understanding of what a table is and its function. So with all that, this person had an idea to build your table, and who knows what other ideas influenced their idea and desire to build the table? But they had the idea, and a bunch of other people helped them gain the resources and see that idea through to fruition.

Also, you had a desire for a table, which came from somewhere, and that particular table was attractive to you, for various reasons due to various conditioning, and then you had the resources to purchase the table and bring it into your home. And somehow, you have a home, which has its own origin story, which involves certain causes and conditions and multiple events. So there were many numerous causes and conditions that landed this table there with you in your home. That is dependent origination. Nothing exists independently in and of itself. But it goes further.

Look at the table itself. If you look at the leg of the table, do you call it a table? No, you say it's the leg. If you look at the top of the table, do you call it the table? Not usually; you say it's the tabletop. There is no singular piece of that table that you call "the table." The table is made up of parts. It is only when all those parts come together that we call it a table. Otherwise we call it something different: leg, side, top, surface. This is what is meant by dependent origination. All things depend on one another.

But self is different, right? Why? The Buddha taught us that self is no different in relationship to dependent origination. Whether you believe it was God, the big bang, or something else altogether that sparked our collective existence, there were nonetheless causes and conditions that landed us here in this body. We didn't just exist; something caused our existence. And aren't we also made up of parts? We are made up of various body parts, plus a brain, plus organs, fluids, tissues, muscles, and so on. And what is so solid about us?

When we refer to our "self" what are we talking about? Sometimes we refer to our body as the self. Sometimes we refer to our mind as the self. Sometimes it's our thought process that we call self, and sometimes it's our pain that we identify as self. And then there are our fixations on "I" and "mine." Is there any solidity to our designations of what is "I," and what is "mine"? Khenchen Thrangu elaborates eloquently:

> We assume that there is "I" and there is "mine," and these are somehow distinct, and yet the distinction between the two does not hold up when we look at how we make it. For example, we commonly think and say "my body." Well, if "my body," is "mine," then it is not an "I," it's something that pertains to or belongs to the "I." If that's the case then the "I" is probably the mind, since the body is something possessed by the "I." Yet sometimes, we think "my mind," in which case the

mind, at the moment, can't be the "I," because it is clearly seen to be the possession of the "I," in which case the "I" must be the body. But before, the "I" was the mind, and the body was its possession. Now the situation is reversed. How is this possible? Let us assume, for the moment, that the "I" is the body. But then we think, "My head hurts." Well, obviously, the "I" must be the body but not the head. Then we think, "My hand hurts." In that case, it's not the hand, either.

If you follow this reasoning, you will discover that there's no clear distinction, practically speaking, between the bases of designation for the concepts "I" and "mine." Some things we sometimes designate as "I," at other times we designate as "mine."[10]

We see in this example that "I" is the owner and "mine" is what is owned, but there is nothing that inherently, independently, and permanently manifests in this way. What's more is that when something is "mine," and something happens to what is "mine," I suffer. The teachings on dependent origin are inseparable from the Buddha's teaching on impermanence. All phenomena, including self, are impermanent. Nothing is permanent. Everything is constantly arising, ceasing, or changing. This was illuminated in Thrangu's teachings as impermanence relates to self—what we call self at one time (the body) is not what we call self at another time (the mind). It changes.

Nothing lasts forever, not even self. The ego's clinging to an idea of a superior, everlasting, solid, permanent self is at the root of all causes of suffering. The Buddha taught that clinging to any form of self, a lower self (the ego), and even a higher self, is grounds for suffering. Attaching ourselves to an eternal self that survives and lives on forever is understandable yet directly related to the ego's fear of death and the unknown. This lack of eternal self is called the "not-self characteristic," or "annata" in Pali.

Diving deeply into the concept of not-self is beyond the scope of this text. However, what it boils down to is an invitation to release our attachments to the desires of self and to explore the fears of self—fear of demise, fear of the unknown. Like the ego, fear is not to be villainized. It is to be attended to, cared for, and healed. While our true nature can be likened to space, and we want space—we say we "need space," and we feel unsettled when we "don't have space" because of trauma or lack of boundaries—we simultaneously fear space because we've been so removed from our nature that it feels like unknown land. And for the ego, space can feel like death, and it's spent its whole life fighting for its survival.

THE SPACE BETWEEN

You may have heard of or read *The Tibetan Book of the Dead* or *The Tibetan Book of Living and Dying*, which was originally written as the *Bardo Thötröl*. "Bardo" means gap. In relation to life and death, it is the intermediate state between the two. The space between. However, the great Buddhist teachers have informed us that the *Bardo Thötröl* has as much to do with living as it does with dying. The bardo is now. It's happening all of the time. It's the space when something has ended, and something else has not yet begun. Impermanence being the way of things, the moment between the last and the next is always here.

I experienced this in a profound way when I left my dance career and had not yet embarked on my yoga and spiritual journey. I experienced it again when I embarked on my spiritual journey and was called to examine my conditioning and decolonize so much of the pain I had internalized. If you reflect on your life, you'll identify many moments of bardo, some small and some incredibly profound. The challenging thing with the space in between is that it is unknown, and therefore, uncomfortable. The space exemplifies the impermanent nature of things—the lack of solidity of self and all phenomena.

It can feel scary, even groundless, like we've lost our footing. When trauma happens, it's against our volition. We did not consent. We're left with this very scary space in between. Something bad happened, and we don't know what's going to happen next. We're scared in the space, and it's fully understandable. We become fearful of our own spacious nature. We forget.

Bringing our pain onto the path is embracing the space in between, leaning into the uncertainty. The space is our nature. If we are having trauma reactions like flashbacks, intrusive thoughts, hypervigilance, and the like, it would not be self-compassionate to force ourselves into that quiet space. If that's the case, we need support, and we may need to work with the trauma in the body in a more active way first. Appendix B offers support to those who are triggered by breath work—the deep breathing, particularly the elongated exhale, can bring up death and fear for some trauma survivors. So honor where you are. But when the space begins to feel more accessible, we can go there. It is in that silent, unknown space that we can really drop into the "now," not the "what was" or "what will be." Presence and unlimited potentiality are in this space. Freedom is in this space. So if you feel ready, let's explore that space.

EMBODIMENT PRACTICE: A MEDITATION ON THE SPACE BETWEEN THE BREATH

Embodiment Preparation

Reading is cerebral and gets us into the thinking, analytical brain, but in meditation, we are looking to be less cerebral and more embodied in the experience. So it's nice to create some space after reading and before meditating.

I invite you to take a moment to move your body. Maybe shake your arms and legs, maybe take a deep breath in and flutter your lips on the breath out, maybe stand up and jump up and down if that's available to you, go for a walk, or even get up to wash your hands and then come back.

> Please remember to utilize the resources in
> Appendices A, B, and C, should you need them.

EMBODIMENT PRACTICE

I invite you to find a comfortable position for your body, lying, sitting, or standing. You could relax your gaze or close your eyes. As you connect your feet to the earth, feel free to call in any spiritual resources that support your journey.

Acknowledge the parts of your body that are connected to the earth. Take a moment to honor this connection, with your awareness, with gratitude, or maybe by taking a slow breath in and out.

Begin to notice your body and what it's holding. If there is tension in the body, imagine that tension relaxing. Send long conscious breaths to that space inside.

Perhaps even move your body in a way that helps it relax further.

If there are places within that won't relax, stay curious about the powerful messages that could be residing there.

Part 1: Breath Anchoring (Shamatha/Mindfulness)

Bring your attention to your lower abdomen.

Try not to change your breath in any way.

Notice the breath in and out.

Begin to focus your attention on the out breath and the gentle movement in the abdomen as the breath exits the body.

Allow your focus to anchor here (on the out breath in the abdomen) for several minutes. If your mind wanders away from the anchor, lovingly return it each time.

Part 2: Elongating the Breath

Begin to consciously lengthen the breath, drawing out each inhalation and exhalation.

Allow the inhalation to inflate the abdomen and then the chest, and the exhalation to leave the chest and then the abdomen.

Breathe this way a bit longer, maybe approaching about 10 breath cycles or so.

Part 3: Expanding the Space

As you continue to breathe, shift your focus to the exhalation. You're still inhaling long and deep, but you're particularly interested in the exhalation. Continue this way for several breath cycles.

Slowly shift your focus to the very end of the exhalation. Continue this way for several breath cycles.

At the end of each exhalation there is a pause, a space before the next inhalation comes.

This is the space between the breath. The space that arrives after the exhalation ends, but before the next inhalation comes. Experience that space.

Imagine that space like a welcoming hammock hanging between two tall, grounded trees.

Imagine your body–mind relaxing into that hammock in the space between the breath.

At the end of each exhalation, gently drop your body–mind into that space.

Continue for as long as you'd like, or at least several more cycles of breath, if you can.

As you're breathing, remain aware: aware of any softness, any spaciousness, any peace you feel.

When it feels complete, consciously exit this practice by relaxing your control of the breath—allowing your breath to return to its natural rhythm and pace.

Take several moments to notice your body–mind. Extend gratitude inward toward your body, if possible.

Feel your body connected to the earth again. Take a moment to again honor this connection, maybe with a breath, an affirmation, or words of gratitude.

Take your time to gently blink the eyes open, if they were closed. Slowly begin to look around, mindfully taking in your surroundings.

Journal or record what you've witnessed and discovered, if it feels right.

※

CLOSING WITH INTENTION

If you've ever found yourself in a moment of deep, quiet introspection, you may have experienced the space. It's a moment when thought and conceptualization are suspended and you find yourself simply resting in the vast awareness that is our true nature.

In meditation, it can seem like a flash of emptiness—space without thought. Literally coming out of nowhere, spontaneously and unexpectedly it arises within the conditions of calm abiding and rest. I invite you to be open to the space, both within and outside your meditation practice.

How does the space tend to manifest for you, in your day to day?

How do you respond to it?

What to Do Next
Deepening the practice: Revisit this meditation. It's a form of shamatha,

or mindfulness practice.[11] In this variation, the space between the breath is our anchor. When our mind wanders to a thought, a story, an emotion, and so on, we acknowledge it and return to the anchor.

However, sometimes the thought, the story, the emotion that enters our mind is not ready to be released. Maybe it's a negative core belief being carried by our inner child (e.g., "I'm unlovable"). Naturally we want to turn away from painful beliefs like that. But this belief is an indicator that a young, injured part of us needs our attention and care. Instead of releasing the belief "I'm unlovable" and returning to the anchor, welcome the belief into the space between the breath. This is welcoming the little inner child home—it's inviting them to practice with you. The painful beliefs they carry will transform in time with your love and care, and I'm offering additional practices to help you with healing these negative core beliefs in the chapters ahead.

For now, when thoughts and feelings arise in meditation, release them and return to the anchor, but if they won't go, if they're not ready to be released, welcome them into the space between the breath, welcome them home.

As we part, I'd like to leave you with these words of the Dzogchen Ponlop Rinpoche:

> Our fundamental nature of mind is a luminous expanse of awareness that is beyond all conceptual fabrication and completely free from the movement of thoughts. It is the union of emptiness and clarity, of space and radiant awareness that is endowed with supreme and immeasurable qualities. From this basic nature of

emptiness everything is expressed; from this everything arises and manifests.[12]

May the healing and benefits obtained by way of these words contribute to the liberation of all beings, living and nonliving, without exception.

3

AWAKENING OUR COMPASSIONATE HEARTS

Love and compassion are necessities, not luxuries.
Without them, humanity cannot survive.

—HIS HOLINESS THE DALAI LAMA,
THE ART OF HAPPINESS[1]

Teachers of the Buddhadharma will often say that, along the path of awakening, just like a bird, we need two wings to fly.[2] These are the wing of wisdom and the wing of compassion. Just as a bird cannot fly with only one wing, we cannot awaken without both wisdom and compassion. In Chapter Two we spoke to our inherent good nature, what we call Buddha Nature. This lives within each of us. Perhaps revisit the words of the Dzogchen Ponlop Rinpoche from the end of Chapter Two, as they illuminate this core essence within.

There is something within each of us that is the same. This is our Buddha Nature. Another of my teachers, Jetsün Khandro Rinpoche, describes this as our "mind's natural inclination toward goodness" or kindness. This basic goodness is the resource that allows both wisdom and compassion to be accessed, nourished, and strengthened. In Buddhism, when we speak to wisdom, we are referring to the understanding that all things are empty (space and awareness), that self is empty, that the mind itself is emptiness plus luminosity. This understanding is called ultimate bodhichitta within the schools of Mahayana Buddhism.

BODHICHITTA: AWAKENED HEART

Around the first century, Buddhism split into two predominant schools that are maintained today: Theravada and Mahayana. The Theravada school existed prior to the Mahayana, dating back to 500 BCE. This path focuses on the individual quest for awakening and following the sutras (teachings) of the Buddha, and may involve meditating on retreat by oneself for years at a time, if not for the remainder of one's life. Meditating on retreat for years is common for monks and ordained people in the Mahayana lineage as well, but there are some key distinctions that set Mahayana apart from Theravada. We'll focus on one of those distinctions.

There are multiple traditions of Buddhism under the Mahayana school, including Zen Buddhism and Tibetan Buddhism (also called Vajrayana). Like the Theravada schools, the Mahayana schools adhere to the sutras but emphasize the bodhisattva path. A person on the bodhisattva path works for their own awakening but also agrees not to walk through the gates of nirvana (absolute freedom) until every other sentient being is also awakened, or free. On the bodhisattva path we will leave no other being behind, not even what we may perceive to be the enemy at first glance.

Guided by the compassion of their hearts, bodhisattvas are awakened beings that choose to remain awake in the world, as the Buddha did, and work toward the liberation of all sentient beings without exception. Without exception? Meaning even the most evil, violent, vicious people are included? Yes. Understanding that we all have Buddha Nature, and that trauma and suffering can obscure that nature but do not destroy it, we understand that each living being, no matter how despicable their behavior, has within them the potential for awakening. And as we are all interconnected, really, none of us are free until all of us are free.

Ultimate bodhichitta, the embodied understanding of the wisdom of emptiness, allows us to go there. If all things and people are empty, there is equality there. There's an understanding that we are all the same. We understand impermanence, that we are all always changing, and this capacity for change means that we can heal, and even the violent ones can change and tap into their innate goodness if they are shown the love they need. Dependent origination reminds us that our life circumstances have landed us in different situations, but in reality, we are more alike than different. Ultimate bodhichitta inspires the understanding that all beings want the same thing—happiness and freedom from suffering.

"Bodhichitta" literally translates as "awakened mind," but as my teacher Karla Jackson-Brewer says, "In Buddhism, the mind is in the heart." Zen teacher Brother Chân Pháp Hải, who trained under Thich Nhat Hanh and worked alongside him for many years, teaches that in the Buddha's time, Vedic times, the seat of consciousness was considered to be in the heart.[3] The Buddha himself was a scientist of his time. What the Buddha taught and what many Vedic sages understood through introspective experience is supported by today's neuroscience. Modern studies have found that the heart has its own brain/nervous system, often called the "little brain" or "heart brain" and is composed of roughly 40,000 neurons that are akin to neurons in the brain.[4] We'll dive into this even more deeply in Chapter Four when we look at the vagus nerve and how this nerve relays messages between the heart and the brain as well as other body organs, making up a critical part of our social engagement and survival systems, as well as our consciousness.

Bodhichitta is our awakened, wise, compassionate heart. There are two types of bodhichitta that resonate with the two wings of the path. Ultimate bodhichitta personifies the wisdom wing—the wisdom of the empty nature of self and all phenomena. Relative bodhichitta breathes life into the wing of compassion. The bodhisattva's decision to awaken, but to remain in the world until every last sentient being is also free, is the essence of relative bodhichitta. Relative bodhichitta is radically awakened compassion.

One of the most influential early Buddhist teachers, an eighth-century Indian master teacher and monk known as Shantideva, is perhaps best known for his text *The Way of the Bodhisattva*. This text outlines, for the ordained and layperson, what is to be cultivated and concentrated should one wish to take the Bodhisattva Vow. The essence of relative bodhichitta is gracefully transmitted by his words:

> For as long as space endures,
> As long as there are beings,
> I will remain to eliminate
> The sufferings of beings.[5]

This is the nature of relative bodhichitta. It's working toward our own liberation, as we simultaneously work for the liberation of all beings, even the ones who have harmed us. Our innate goodness allows us to easily feel compassion for the ones we find it easy to love, but it's hard for us to extend compassion to the ones we find it hard to love. Bodhichitta is the ability to extend compassion indiscriminately. This is compassion at its most radical. The two bodhichittas, ultimate and relative, are inseparable from and uplift one another. Tapping into ultimate bodhichitta, emptiness, gives birth to the radical compassion that is relative bodhichitta.

THE BODHISATTVA DECISION

The decision to awaken our compassionate hearts is a privilege and an honor. It's a decision not to waste this life on ourselves alone. It's a decision to suffer less, by working to release ourselves from the karmic tendencies and defilements of our own egocentric existence.[6] With the bodhisattva decision, to remain awake in the world until all sentient beings are free, comes a sense of purposefulness that is immediately liberative.

I personally chose to take the Bodhisattva Vow. And when I first prepared to do so within a spiritual community based in Colorado, parts of me were horrified. I was met with the unresolved trauma and fears of my own body–mind around what taking such a radical oath, so contradictory to the values of the individualistic culture in which I live, might mean for me. Parts of me were scared: "What if I mess up?" "What if I am not nice all the time?" But I worked with those fears and became grounded in the understanding that the Bodhisattva Vow is not about being perfect; it's about being devoted to living more and more into our true nature: awake, loving, active in the world.

You don't have to take a formal Bodhisattva Vow with a Buddhist sangha to make the decision to live with the purpose of alleviating suffering for all beings. This "coming to" can flourish in its own way that resonates with you. I will share that after taking the vow, it was as though something within me immediately lightened. And for the next three days I didn't really get mad at anybody. On day four, my humanness was activated, and something ticked me off—I have no memory of what. But the vow is not about having no emotions; it's about what we do with them. To bring our pain onto the path—that is the promise we're making. Befriending and turning toward our pain, and that of others—that's the vow. It starts with a personal promise to ourselves: "I'm going to suffer less. I'm going to be free." It continues with a promise to the world: "I'm going to help you suffer less. I'm going to help you be free."

AN AFRIKAN BIRTH STORY

The bodhisattva way and bodhichitta are about love and service. I'd like to encapsulate for you another beautiful story, presented by Malidoma Patrice Somé in *The Healing Wisdom of Africa* that also speaks to this gift.

The Dagara people, like many Afrikans practicing earth-centered religions, believe that we negotiate our soul's purpose with the elders of the spirit world prior to our birth. When the council of elders has agreed that the life purpose we've presented is the right fit, we are allowed into bodily form. Conception is sacred and when an expecting person learns they are pregnant, the entire village celebrates with a timely ritual.[7]

The tribe wonders, "What purpose does this soul, choosing to incarnate into human form, wish to share with our community? Why is this ancestor choosing to incarnate now?" It goes without saying that this unborn child has chosen to come into the village to be of service and contribute to the collective good, and this sparks an enthusiasm in the villagers. The expecting mother and a village shaman are placed at the center of the village celebration. The shaman has the ability to contact the spirit world and, on this occasion, does so to communicate with the soul of the unborn child and learn of its soulful purpose for coming earthside.

It is understood that each person's purpose is profoundly meaningful in cultivating a healthy sense of individual identity and, in turn, in keeping up a spiritually focused and harmonious community. Once the shaman gains access to the message, they share it with the childbearing person and villagers. The entire village celebrates the purpose of this unborn child, lovingly supports the childbearing person, and excitedly awaits the birth.

In this tradition, similarly to many Eastern traditions, it is believed that the process of being born itself creates an amnesia, and we lose sight of who we are and our purpose for coming here. Yet our community remembers for us. After all, the entire village was there to celebrate our soulful purpose just months before our birth. When the new baby is born, the entire village again celebrates this new member of the community.

The entire community continues to nurture and foster the growth of this child as they enter the world, supporting them in staying connected to their purpose as they grow and develop. In supporting the individual in living a life of service, as destined by their purpose, and thus nurturing a healthy sense of identity, the community supports the child's mental, emotional, physical, and spiritual development—and, in turn, their ability to transcend their individual identity and reach a higher spiritual plane. This, in turn, benefits the community as a whole, since any individual's purpose is always that of service or giving back to the community in some way. This supports the collective purpose in Indigenous Afrikan living—spiritual progression.

As life happens and trauma occurs, it's not uncommon that a spiritual crisis of sorts will arrive. A child or adolescent may feel lost or misdirected. But as the entire village was there to celebrate this child's higher purpose from the beginning, the community resolves to help the child remember and guides them back on track. Not only is service emphasized, but this intimate community is a healing resource to support each being in the aftermath of something painful.

There is medicine in this system. It's different but parallel to the bodhisattva path. Allowing life to be about more than ourselves brings a release from deep within. There's a deep knowing that our liberation is tied together. No one is free until all of us are free.

COMPASSION IS ACTION

My favorite definition of compassion is simple, yet I found it profound. It comes from a sacred Tibetan Buddhist text called *The Six Perfections.*[8] Here compassion is defined as "finding it unbearable to see others suffer or create the causes of suffering." What I found compelling about this definition was the use of the word "unbearable." It's a charged word.

As a trauma therapist, the majority of the people I see have been through that which was unbearable. Life at present may even feel so.

When our nervous systems experience that which is unbearable, it sends us into a state of shutdown, also called immobilization, meaning we can't move or mobilize. Our bodies, and sometimes much of our identity, becomes frozen in time.

Compassion, however, is not related to our experience in the moment when something traumatic is happening to us, as much as it relates to when we are in a witnessing role. When we are no longer in a trauma response (fight, flight, or immobilization), as we navigate the world, we both experience and we witness. We may witness others in pain, or we may witness ourselves in pain. When we witness others in pain and remain a witness, there's some sort of trauma response happening inside. We're immobilized—our hearts are closed off. But when we can mobilize beyond the witnessing state and act to relieve the pain, that is compassion.

"Unbearable" inspires action. When we witness others or self in pain, this unbearableness drives us to act to end the suffering we are witnessing. Remember, ultimate bodhichitta informs relative bodhichitta. Compassion does not discriminate. True compassion is born from the field of equanimity. It's not, "Okay, I am going to help alleviate your suffering because you look like me. We're the same race, or age, or gender, or we have the same hobbies." That's a response informed by the ego's sense of separateness: "I'll divvy out compassion to you, and you, but not you."

Authentic compassion is extended to everyone, all beings, simply because they are.

✳

BARRIERS TO COMPASSION

There is something within each of us that is the same. Sometimes it's hard to see this. The appearance of separation is a response to trauma. When we are hurt, we want to protect our heart—put a barricade around it, not let too much in. Trauma can distance us from our heart. There is a neurological explanation to this, which we'll dive into in Chapter Four. Trauma creates a separateness inside. Trauma is stored in multiple areas of the brain, fragmented, like a puzzle whose pieces are scattered about. Trauma is stored in the muscles and connective tissue of the body in the form of body memory, tension, and somatic pain.

Trauma creates energetic blockages and can also pose a spiritual crisis. Trauma creates polarizations inside. The result is that we develop many protective parts of us that seek to keep the memories of the trauma far away. These parts of us push the trauma away from our consciousness, but they also push down our inclination toward compassion, because all of it is within the body.

Trauma lends itself to disembodiment. To be compassionate toward oneself or another, to work to remove suffering, we must have worked with our own nervous system enough that we can stay embodied. If we dissociate or shut down, we cannot act. So we heal and train our nervous systems to look at suffering slowly. Our window of tolerance, the amount of distress our nervous system can tolerate before having a trauma response, expands.[9] In time, we can include more and more in our lives. We can include the parts of us holding the pain, and we can include others and their pain, without shutting down. Compassion is a willingness to include. It's embodied inclusivity.

If we tend to extend love and care to those who are like us and struggle to offer it to people we perceive as not like us, it's also likely that we struggle to show compassion toward all parts of ourselves. It's easy to uplift the parts of us we like, but how do we treat the parts of us that we don't?

＊

REPROGRAMMING THE BODY-MIND TOWARD COMPASSION

So here comes this idea again of looking directly at our suffering. The parts of us that like to push it all down, numb, distance, and escape may be doing somersaults inside you right now, and that's okay. Here's another invitation to take note of any resistance, fear, concern, or hesitation that's arising. We all have parts of us that inhibit our ability to extend bodhichitta, radical compassion, inward and outward. These parts of us have their own story that needs to be witnessed. These parts themselves need our compassion. So take note, because these may be some of the first parts you explore in the embodiment practices to come.

In order to get through it, you've got to go to it. Bringing our pain onto the path is the conscious decision to do something different. To turn toward the injury inside. To stop overidentifying with our pain—to care for it, befriend it, and allow it to transform into something else when it's ready.

This notion of bringing our pain onto the path is not a breakthrough idea. It's been around for as long as people have existed. Many Indigenous Afrikan communities, as well as other Indigenous communities around the world, have long used pain intentionally as a vehicle for evolution by way of rituals and initiations. The ascetics in India's Vedic times used physical pain as a means for spiritual liberation. Running away from pain is modern and cultural.

In Mahayana schools, it's understood that without bodhichitta we cannot awaken. So within these traditions the bodhisattva path is at the core and, with this, so is mind training. Jetsün Khandro Rinpoche explains that the term "mind training" is not to be taken harshly—this is not about taming your mind like it's some type of beast. It's not about force.[10] This is actually a gentle approach where we turn inward to recognize the good, pristine, wise, awake nature that our mind already has. We are already a buddha, already awake.

It's just that we've forgotten how to live like we are. We've come to believe we are something else. Khandro Rinpoche explains that these mind-training teachings are about "tapping into our innate compassion and wisdom"—our wings.

There are various practices of mind training, the most popular perhaps being the lojong teachings, which were brought to Tibet by the great 10th-century Indian Buddhist master teacher Atisha. These teachings were received and compiled into an accessible format by the Tibetan teacher Geshe Chekawa into seven areas (called seven points of mind) and 59 slogans that help us come to understand the true meaning of what it takes to be a bodhisattva. Today, many Eastern and Western Buddhist practitioners study and meditate on these 59 slogans on their personal journeys of awakening.

And what is so profound about these mind-training teachings? They invite us to go against our survival instinct of pushing pain out. As Buddhist teacher Kate Johnson puts it, "One of the things that can get in the way of us showing up for one another's liberation, is the habitual human tendency to recoil in the face of suffering, to turn away from it."[11] The lojong teachings guide us to be with and turn toward that from which we usually retreat. And there's something more. They invite us to reverse our egocentric tendency of elevating our own survival over that of others.

With these lojong teachings, we are guided to practice giving up what is most precious to us, offering it to another, knowing we all really want the same things. One of the most popular texts on the lojong practice, *The Great Path of Awakening*, was written by the 19th-century Tibetan Buddhist scholar Jamgon Kongtrul. In translator Ken McLeod's introduction to the text, he explains, "In this system, one's way of experiencing situations in everyday life is transformed into the way a bodhisattva might experience those situations."[12]

Lojong is essentially about befriending pain, getting to know it. And with this we receive the gift of watching pain transform. Lojong is equally about offering to others what we most treasure and take comfort in. The teachings invite us to lessen the grip of our ego and awaken our compassionate hearts. With this, the teachings illuminate for us the parts of us that cling, that fear, that hate, that hide, that struggle to be generous, loving, and kind. All is revealed when we begin to put these teachings into practice. The resistance we feel toward sending others healing and well-being, particularly the people or groups we find it hard to love, indicates that there are parts of us inside who are burdened and who desperately need our care and attention. When we can't give, it's because something inside of us needs us to give to it first. It needs our time and our love.

At the heart of all the various mind-training vehicles is a meditative practice called tonglen. Perhaps you've heard of it or have even practiced some variation of it. "Tonglen" is a Tibetan word that means sending and receiving. We'll explore several variations of this practice together shortly. Tonglen is the practice of expanding and opening our hearts, both to our own pain and suffering and to that of the world. This is the receiving. And it's a practice in sending out the very qualities that we wish for, like love, safety, wholeness, freedom. This is the sending. And we eventually allow ourselves to receive in return the qualities we wish for, but we practice giving them away first—sending them out. And our ego may protest. Our shadows will appear. So then we work with the ego in a loving way. We receive, we breathe in, the ego's fear, or disgust, or contempt, and we still practice sending out love even while receiving fear. This is just a sneak peek. All will be revealed.

ANGER IS ALSO WELCOME

Where is the space for anger? That space is here too. The Buddha taught that all is welcome—there need not be an aversion to anything. Anger and the dark side of our emotional experience holds its own wisdom. Anger is informed by a sense that there is an injustice happening around or within. Being awake in the world means we are awake to the injustices happening in the world. And in a culture that celebrates separateness, one that was founded on the blood of people in Black and Brown bodies, there is a legacy of injustice and separateness that many traumatized, disembodied folx are fighting to sustain to this day.

It makes sense to be angry. James Baldwin spoke with passion when he said that "to be [Black] in this country and to be relatively conscious is to be in a state of rage almost all of the time."[13] This path is not about avoiding the real, human emotions like anger and rage. My teacher Lama Rod Owens says that if we don't feed our anger, it will consume us. It will eat us alive.

In his book *Love and Rage: The Path of Liberation Through Anger*, Lama Rod Owens teaches how when accompanied by love, rage can mobilize us to act—to act to end suffering. His book recounts an interview he did with Kate Johnson where he speaks to this opportunity anger proposes: "What I began to see was that my anger was valid, and that it was trying to teach me. Anger is actually pointing to a really real kind of woundedness, of hurt. Look at what the anger is pointing to."[14] Anger can actually point us toward self-compassion, illuminating the parts of us that need care, if we're willing to look at the hurt within and work to remove that hurt.

Anger, when accompanied by compassion, is a form of wisdom. But if we only have the anger and we don't have the compassion, the anger is like a poison inside our bodies. It kills us slowly. And it keeps us in shackles. The ones who want to harm us want us to be angry, want us to suffer, because they're suffering, but when we hold compassion with our anger, or compassion without anger, we are doing something liberative, radical, and transformative. To resist being poisoned by others' suffering is a form of resistance, and to maintain our bodhichitta in spite of it is radical compassion indeed.

Perhaps most radical is the idea of equanimity—of showing compassion to the violent ones that want to hurt us. This is something that may take time, especially if we're experiencing the abusive force of a perpetrator in our current living situation or daily life. So receive this teaching only when and if you are ready.

Suffering begets more suffering; people who are hurting hurt other people. Hurt and suffering have been passed down generationally and passed around in our society for over a millennium.

What is going on inside the body–minds of those who perpetrate harm? Are they embodied? Are they joyful? Are they connected to their true nature? Are they free? No. When people are doing harm, they are filled with their own suffering on the inside.

When someone does me harm, and I'm awake enough to know it's because of their own suffering, and I've decided to embark on this journey of being a compassionate vehicle for change in this world, then I will see all suffering as unbearable—not some suffering. This is equanimity. All of it is equal—ultimate bodhichitta. We don't prioritize the suffering of the ones whom we find it easy to love above the suffering of the ones we find it hard to love. We don't perpetuate the hierarchy. The trauma of separateness ends with us.

I'm not talking about putting ourselves in life-threatening situations where people who hate us may have the opportunity to harm us. I am talking about energetically sending compassion to the ones who are creating the most suffering, the same way you would send the innocent child compassion without holding back. It's counterintuitive. There may be parts of you who are feeling all types of resistance to this idea. But I invite you to entertain it for a minute. What if we had compassion for the ones who were doing the most harm, perpetuating so much suffering? What if we could remove their suffering? Would there then not be a lot less suffering in the world?

I can only speak for myself, but for me, as a Black woman, in a white supremacy–driven world, when I get to embody compassion with anger, or compassion as opposed to anger, I am choosing my own freedom—

and that is radical. It's something I invite you to sit with. Take note of the parts of you that feel resistance toward this idea. Where do they show up in your body (what physical sensations of discomfort do you feel)? And what emotions are these parts of you carrying? Hold them with grace. Bring this into tonglen meditation with you. That's what we can do. Bring it onto the path. Pain is alchemizing. Let's work with it, not against it.

EMBODIMENT PRACTICE: TONGLEN, SENDING AND RECEIVING

Embodiment Preparation

Tonglen, sending and receiving, is the embodiment component of lojong mind training. With our ego-clinging tendencies, progression through the stages of this practice challenges us spiritually and illuminates for us where we are extra attached to what we believe to be ours. So we'll take it slowly, and we'll go for four rounds. You could also focus on one round per sitting, if that makes the practice more accessible.

First, we'll practice tonglen for ourselves as a way to be with whatever pain or resistance (physical, mental, emotional) is showing up in our body–mind. We'll breathe with this pain, and we won't rush to find a remedy for it. Take note of how you react to this, and hold it all with grace and compassion if you can.

Second, we'll practice dropping the subject (us), the object (the thing that we believed caused the pain), and the entire story of our pain. We'll instead tap into the feeling of the pain itself. We'll practice connecting to another person who also knows this same pain. We'll breathe to remove their pain, and we'll breathe to send them the antidote to their pain.

Third, we'll tap into people all over the world who carry this same pain, and we'll practice in a way similar to the second round.

Last, we'll focus on the antidote. We'll send and receive the antidote, both for ourselves and for the entire collective.

> Note that tonglen does include intentional breathwork. If deep breathing is unsettling to your nervous system, feel free to breathe naturally instead (the way you breathe without thinking about it), or turn to Appendix B and/or C for support.

EMBODIMENT PRACTICE

I invite you to find a comfortable position for your body—lying, sitting, or standing. Take a moment to observe the parts of your body that are connected to the earth (floor). As you nourish this connection, feel free to call in any spiritual resources that support your journey.

I invite us to consciously generate bodhichitta—a heart-centered intention to embody compassion and to be of service, to remove suffering within.

Feel free to practice the Space Between the Breath meditation from Chapter Two first, so that you can drop in and get centered.

Begin to breathe deeply in and out through your nose or mouth.

Round One

Become aware of what pain, tension, or discomfort you are carrying in your body–mind. Maybe it's a physical sensation and/or an emotion, and/or a belief or a fear. Observe it.

As you inhale deeply, imagine breathing in that pain. You're welcoming it.

As you breathe out deeply, rest. Try not to push the pain away. Just relax your focus on it a bit and imagine your body relaxing into the earth.

Continue this. Inhale, breathe it in. Exhale, relax into it. Try not to push it away. Open your heart to it. Listen to it.

Continue this for 1 to 5 minutes or more. Notice your body–mind.

Round Two

Drop the "my," to this pain. And drop the story you hold around it.

Bring to mind someone (a loved one, a neutral person, or a stranger) that also holds this same type of pain (heartbreak, grief, loneliness, fear, etc.).

See an image of that person in front of you.

Breathe in deeply and think about drawing their pain out of their body and into the compassionate light at your heart. *Let it transform at your heart.*

Breathe out deeply, and send this person the antidote to their suffering—whatever they need (e.g., love, feeling seen, wholeness, monetary resources). Let their body fill with the antidote.

Continue this for 1 to 5 minutes or more. Notice your body–mind.

Round Three

Still looking at this person in front of you, think about all the people all over the world who hold this same pain that you know and this person knows.

Invite an image that represents all of these people to come in front of you.

As in Round Two, breathe in deeply and imagine drawing the suffering away from this collective of people and into the healing power of your heart. *Let it transform at your heart.*

Breathe out deeply and send out the antidote.

Continue this for 1 to 5 minutes or more. Notice your body–mind.

Round Four

Allow your attention to focus on the antidote. Begin to breathe in and out the antidote to the suffering you and this collective are carrying.

Send and receive the antidote, riding the breath. They receive it and you receive it.

Continue this for 1 to 5 minutes or more. Notice your body–mind.

Closing

Take your time to slowly and gently dissolve this practice. End perhaps by offering gratitude, connecting your feet to the land, or calling in your spiritual resources again.

Take some time to journal and reflect. Be gentle with your tender heart.

CLOSING WITH INTENTION

How did that go for you? All is welcome. It's not uncommon for people to struggle with the idea of welcoming their pain. It's important to understand welcoming as a form of acceptance.

Acceptance is different from agreeing with the causes that created your pain. You can know there was an injustice and still accept that the pain is there. Acceptance is acknowledging reality as it is. It's saying, "Okay, this pain is here now." It's a form of equanimity. We're not attached to it, but we're also not avoiding the pain.

We may fear that welcoming our pain will make it stay or become stronger. In fact, quite the opposite—welcoming transforms it. What we see as an inner enemy is often a vulnerable, scared part of us that needs our care. Sometimes it's our inner child holding a painful burden from which it seeks liberation. When these parts of us get what they need (love, care, to have a voice), they soften. This is the medicine in turning toward our pain rather than away.

Another place where people get caught up is welcoming other people's pain into their own hearts. It's important to remember that all things are impermanent; nothing is going to stay there. But we're not literally adopting people's pain—we're inviting our own potential for buddhahood, our bodhichitta, to transform the pain right at our heart space. A part of you may still feel resistant toward this, and that's okay. If that's the case, I invite you to work with this resistant part when we get to Chapter Five, on the internal family systems model of psychotherapy.

I invite you to return to the practices in this chapter and in Chapter

Two often. To continue to reflect and journal. To hold yourself with grace and offer compassion inward whenever you can.

May the healing and benefits obtained by way of these words contribute to the liberation of all beings, living and nonliving, without exception.

WIRED FOR AWAKENING

The Neurobiology of Compassion

We listen to the sounds of words before we look for the meanings of those words. Autonomic listening is inextricably linked with the need for self-compassion.

—DEB DANA, *ANCHORED*[1]

We are always in a perpetual state of being created and creating ourselves.

—DANIEL J. SIEGEL, *THE DEVELOPING MIND*[2]

REVERENCE PRACTICE

There is no Western model of psychotherapy or methodology for understanding human behavior that has not been informed by earlier Indigenous people, even when those Indigenous humans are dis- or miscredited. As a psychotherapist who lives and trained in the West, I practice and believe in the psychotherapeutic modalities I use to support the healing of myself and others. However, I feel compelled to make explicit here that while modern Western science has been privileged in our postcolonial world, Indigenous people of color were the first to support trauma healing in a way that was holistic and human centered. Therefore, before moving forward into the neuroscience that many of us deeply enjoy, myself included, I'd like to invite us to pay homage and extend gratitude to the Indigenous ancestors of the land we occupy, as well as the living Indigenous people around the world, from Africa, to Asia, to Europe, to South and North America, to Australia and Antarctica alike, for their lives, their voices, their wisdom, and their voluntary and involuntary sacrifices.

We spoke to our inherent basic goodness, the Buddha Nature that resides in each of us. The aspiration to embody bodhichitta, compassion in its most radical form that extends itself without discrimination to help all beings become free, can offer us a sense of purpose and help ease our suffering. Yet disembodiment and separation are a natural consequence of trauma. The appearance of separation is a trauma response. It could be said that trauma enlivens the ego—exaggerating this sense of self and other.

Trauma creates layers of nervous system reactivity that make it more challenging to embody bodhichitta, radical compassion. In this chapter we'll look at why and how this is as we explore the neurobiology of trauma and compassion, in tandem. Tapping into our capacity for self-compassion is foundational in our healing process. And fortunately, compassion is our true nature. There is something inside that trauma cannot damage, and this is our own awakening, compassionate heart.

THE MIND IS IN THE HEART

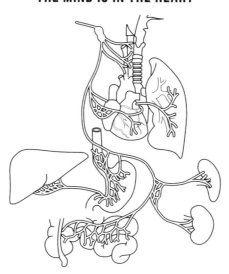

Figure 4.1 Full vagus nerve displaying both pathways

In our bodies there is a long nerve that makes up a very important part of our nervous system. This nerve is typically called the vagus nerve by Westerners, but I am going to join somatic psychotherapist and author Resmaa Menakem in calling it the *soul nerve*.[3] From a neurobiological perspective, the soul nerve enables the body–mind–heart connection.

It originates at our brain stem, also called the reptilian brain, which is the oldest part of our brain, located in the lower back portion of the skull. Our brain stem is responsible for our survival instincts and motivational drives—"I am thirsty; I need water," "I am hungry; I need food," "I sense desire; I need sex," "All is good; I am safe," "All is not good; I am not safe." The brain stem correlates with our impulsive, automatic, and involuntary behaviors.

From its origin at the brain stem, the soul nerve branches out into two pathways. The ventral pathway connects to the muscles of the face and middle ear, and runs down the back of the throat, bypassing the pharynx and larynx, as well as the heart and lungs. The dorsal pathway connects to the stomach, kidneys, bladder, small and large intestines, colon, spleen, pancreas, and liver. As you can see, the soul nerve, with its ventral and dorsal branches, passes through many of the major organs vital to our functioning and relays messages to the brain about the body's general level of "okayness." In our day-to-day lives, when all is well, the ventral vagal branch creates a state of homeostasis in the body for optimal health, enabling the dorsal vagal branch to support our healthy digestion.[4]

Through a process called neuroception, the soul nerve receives information about the internal environment and delivers this information to the brain. For example, if our bodies are running low on fuel and our stomachs are close to empty, by way of the dorsal branch the stomach sends this message to the brain stem, and the brain stem interprets this as, "I am hungry; I need food." Through the body, the soul nerve also receives input about the external environment. If things in the external environment are safe, our organ functioning remains steady, and no negative signals are sent to the brain stem, thus the message "All is good; I am safe" is felt. If things are unsafe, though, our organ functioning will respond to the external cues in the environment and deliver this information to the brain stem.

When we initially detect a threat, for example, we may stop breathing for a moment (lung activity changes abruptly), and then our heart rate quickens, we may feel a lump in our throat, and our gastrointestinal organs are no longer working to digest our food. In a matter of milliseconds, via the soul nerve, information travels from the gastrointestinal organs, the throat, the lungs, and the heart to the brain stem, and the brain stem recognizes, "All is not good. I am not safe." This is the neurobiological foundation of the age-old adage, "Trust your gut."

Knowing whether or not we are "good" is vital to our survival, and the soul nerve plays a major role with this. The soul nerve, at its optimal function, is concerned with not only our own safety but the safety of others too. There are two primal drivers constantly at work within our system: the desire to be safe and survive, and the desire to connect with others.[5] Ideally, these two needs are in alignment, and we can connect with others while also feeling safe. When these two bio–spiritual needs are in disharmony because we cannot safely connect, the body's drive to survive overcomes the heart's need to relay and relate.

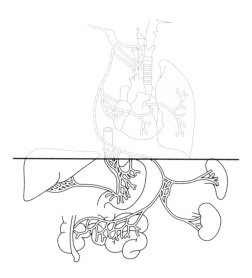

Figure 4.2 Dorsal branch of the vagus nerve

Earlier we spoke about the way that the two branches of the soul nerve, ventral and dorsal, innervate through the body and past many of the vital organs. The older branch of the soul nerve, the dorsal vagal branch, is the part of the soul nerve that bypasses the organs below the diaphragm. This dorsal branch is responsible for the immobilization trauma response. We also refer to this as shutdown or freeze with collapse. The survival mechanism here is to disappear and disengage. The dorsal branch of the soul nerve is present in reptiles and mammals alike, dating back to 500 million years ago.[6] Think about how, when reptiles are faced with threat, they freeze or even feign death until the threat is removed.

When I was young, we lived in Okinawa, Japan, for three years, and we had the cutest "baby" geckos, which seemed to always be inside our home. My older sister, my two younger brothers, and I loved living with these little friends, but the geckos naturally didn't feel the same way about us. When we would walk up to one to say hello, it would pause halfway up the wall in full immobilization response until we were done with our greeting and our parents ushered us into the next activity. The geckos' bodies went into dorsal response—immobile, playing dead. This was their automatic survival instinct. The dorsal branch of the vagus nerve in humans operates in the same way.

When we enter a state of immobilization, we go there involuntarily. Things literally begin to shut down inside as our body prepares for death. This dorsal state is our body's energy conservation system. Here in dorsal our organ functioning declines and our breathing slows, as does our heart rate. Our body stops working to digest the food we've eaten. In this protective response, if we are being physically attacked we may not feel pain. This is a state that many survivors of childhood neglect and abuse drop into at the time of the abuse, and one they may involuntarily reenter often in adulthood, should the trauma of the abuse remain unresolved (think back to Talia in Chapter One).

You may already be considering the problems that could result when brought to this state by trauma that we actually survive. Whenever a new psychotherapy client comes in and tells me they have gastrointestinal issues, I make a mental note that their body may be stuck in immo-bilization. As the therapeutic relationship grows, and we eventually begin to approach the trauma, it often unfolds that this person indeed survived trauma that lent itself to a state of shutdown—their body never updated that the threat had dissipated, so they continue to live from this immobilized place. Fortunately, there are many healing methods we can use to mobilize this stuck energy from the body, and you abso-lutely do not have to reexperience or relive the trauma to do so. This is the intention behind the practices I offer in this book—to support mobilizing the stuck energy in the body through breath work, somatic experience, and/or movement.

OUR SOULFUL SOCIAL ENGAGEMENT SYSTEM

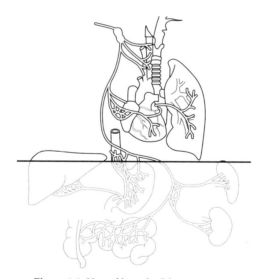

Figure 4.3 Ventral branch of the vagus nerve

While the dorsal pathway bypasses the organs below the diaphragm, the ventral vagal branch bypasses organs above the diaphragm. The ventral branch regulates the heartbeat as well as the muscles that control the face and eyes, the middle ear, the throat (pharynx), and the vocal cords (larynx).[7] This branch of the soul nerve is an integral part of our social engagement system (SES).[8] Ventral is the emergent field for soulful social engagement, characterized by open-heartedness, attunement, intimacy, and love. From this grounded space, we can connect emotionally to others, extend compassion both inward and outward, and feel a sense of unity, a joining with the person across from us. Here, the thrall of our ego is quieted, and our hearts lead the way. This is the nervous system space from which bodhichitta (ultimate and relative) arises.

To create the SES, the soul nerve, which is our 10th cranial nerve, links with several other cranial nerves that control the face, nose, throat, mouth, middle ear, and upper-body motor function (such as tilting the head and shrugging the shoulders).

This is why, when we are talking to a dear friend and we see their facial expression change from one suggesting ease to one of sorrow, we get a sense that something painful is coming up for them. Before our consciousness ever has the chance to interpret what's wrong, we just get it. This is the "heart–brain" we referred to in Chapter Three. We may unconsciously tilt our head to the side and lean in, and with a gentle, soothing voice offer our support. Our nervous system is aligned with our friend's, and we experience this inner knowing of their experience. This is the SES in effective action.

The SES helps us register the heartbreaking, gut-wrenching emotions, the happy and calm emotions, and the shift in between them—it is what allows us to emotionally attune to one another. When in ventral we can identify another's level of okayness not only visually but also through sound. The middle ear filters out background noise to detect the human voice and conversational tone and pitch. If we are talking to a loved one over the phone, our middle ear may detect their voice crack or throat go dry, and our SES informs us that our loved one is about to cry. When we observe visually or audibly a shift in someone, we will likely feel a surge of energy through our own body, perhaps similar to what the other person is feeling, and our nervous systems align. This is what Jetsün Khandro refers to as our innate goodness. We are wired for compassion. We will likely respond to our loved one with care and support, validate their feelings, or try to reassure them that everything will be okay. We are helping this person survive their pain through the love and support we are offering them.

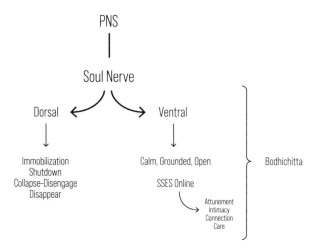

Figure 4.4 Parasympathetic Overview: Bodhichitta Version

The soul nerve is the primary constituent of the parasympathetic nervous system (PNS). Both of its branches, then, dorsal and ventral, relate to PNS states. The PNS is what many of us learned in grade school as "rest and digest." It doesn't matter if we are in ventral and socially engaging or if we are in dorsal and shutting down, when we are ventral dominant or dorsal dominant it is our PNS that is in a role of governance. What we experience on the inside and how we relate to others, though, look and feel very different from ventral to dorsal.

✳

VENTRAL: AN EMBODIED, AWAKENED STATE

You may have already concluded on your own that ventral sounds like a nice place to be. I liken it to a playground where our hearts and souls can run wild and free. In this parasympathetic state we are connected to our hearts—we can soulfully socially engage and share meaningful experiences with others. We may experience a sense of groundedness, peace, calm, presence, or attunement that benefits all we come into contact with. And from this we can turn the light of bodhichitta back inward and extend compassion and grace to ourselves.

Early in my healing journey, meditation was so impactful because it elevated me to a blissful state of consciousness that I had seldom reached previously—a warm, fuzzy openheartedness would sponta-neously emerge from within. In this uninhibited space, free from roam-ing thought, I felt a deep sense of connection not only to myself but to the world. Meditation practices help us access this state. When we talk about emptiness, true nature, bodhichitta, and compassion, it's from this ventral way of being that all of this is available to us.

In "trauma speak," this ability to ground ourselves in ventral is called self-regulation. We can self-regulate to calm our system, but we can also self-regulate to calm others' systems. As our nervous systems feed off one another, one grounded system helps to ground other sys-tems. This is called coregulation. Self-regulation practices are those that we do inside, that bring our activated system back to a ventral state. The practices in this book are practices in self-regulation.

Coregulation is what we do when we have a calm system and help another system to calm. This is what we are called to do as parents, for our children, or as helping professionals, for those we help. When we have a system that can return to ventral most of the time, we bring that energy to the world. Have you ever been in the presence of someone who is very grounded and noticed that when around them you also feel more grounded and peaceful within? This is coregulation at its finest.

I invite you to view all of this information through a lens of equanimity. Just as we don't want to exalt parts of ourselves over others, just as we don't want to denigrate the ego as "bad," we don't have to think of ventral as superior and the other nervous system states as inferior to it. There is a usefulness to all of them. Moreover, staying in ventral and never moving into a sympathetic fight–flight–active freeze response, or a parasympathetic dorsal state of shutdown response, is unrealistic.

In a normal day, one free of violent or terrifying experiences, we are still going to be met with moments of fight or flight and moments of shutdown. We bump into someone at the grocery store—perhaps we go into fight–flight–active freeze momentarily. As long as our system is able to return to ventral with ease, it's not a big deal. Our partner says something, and it activates a part of us that feels unworthy—perhaps we go into shutdown momentarily. As long as our system is able to return to ventral with ease, it's not a big deal. The bigger deal comes when we've accumulated so much trauma in our body that we cannot return to ventral with ease, and little life mishaps become major disturbances.

The healing intention is that we progress our nervous system to a place where, when we are sent into fight–flight–active freeze or shutdown, we can recover and quickly return to ventral with some level of ease. We can be activated, but we can return to ventral, again and again, with less and less effort, because we've befriended and shown care toward the parts of us that feel threatened and activated in the world (the parts carrying the trauma memories, fear, and negative core beliefs about self).

To review, regardless of whether we are in ventral regulation or dorsal shutdown, we are in a parasympathetic nervous system response.

However, within the parasympathetic state of ventral, our social engagement system is fully online. This is where compassion and wisdom have the space to emerge. On the other hand, within the parasympathetic state of dorsal, or immobilization response, we are shut down, and the SES is fully offline. That's an important piece to understand—when we are in shutdown mode, which is an involuntary trauma response, we are unable to effectively socially engage—we're not relational. This means no attunement to others—no registering the heartbreaking, gut-wrenching emotions, no allowance for the flow of love or compassion.

In the trauma field, we say that immobilization is at the root of most traumas. When I say that trauma closes our hearts, this is what I mean. In immobilization response, our SES is offline; we cannot fully connect from our heart space. We are in a mode of protection or disconnection. Intimacy, vulnerability, love, and compassion are not the body's focus—survival is.

Ocean's (she/they) system knew dorsal well. Growing up, their father used love like a weapon, giving it briefly only to take it away, again and again. As an adolescent, a part of her learned to cope with alcohol. In adulthood she continued what she called her "numbing ritual," after she would have an argument with her wife. With alcohol, Ocean could control when and how they went into this shutdown place of collapse and disappear. Yet, in the darkness of intoxication, Ocean would get too close to their unresolved negative core beliefs: "I'm damaged"; "I'm unlovable"; "There is no light within." Too much time in this obscure, shadowy place would land Ocean in a deep depression, another painful dorsal state. But this state

felt familiar, Ocean told me. They overidentified with this state of despair. A part of them, they said, couldn't imagine not having this state—it offered them a reason to go and hide inside, where they couldn't be hurt by the world. But Ocean came to therapy because they sensed there was more for them. While the alcohol muted the darkness, it also muted the light.

Like Ocean, we may find some sense of security in dorsal—parts of us may have learned to collapse when things get hard. And yet living, using this human life to its fullest, is about connecting—being awake and actively present in this world. We are always participating in the world—we can't not participate. But in dorsal, we are removed from our power to contribute. This births a cycle where we feel bad, so we don't participate, and then we feel bad about not participating. Short-term, dorsal can feel cozy to some parts of us, but long-term, it is rarely a satisfying place to reside.

POLYVAGAL THEORY, RELATIONSHIPS, AND REPAIR

My understandings of Polyvagal Theory (PVT) have been informed by its founder, Dr. Stephen Porges, as well as Deb Dana, a psychotherapist and founding member of the Polyvagal Institute. Dana has increased the accessibility of PVT, expanding it beyond the walls of the research laboratory and providing a framework for applying the theory to real-world relationships.

Polyvagal Theory, now a widely recognized and research-supported methodology, was formulated by Dr. Porges and first presented in the literature in 1995.[9] The theory has informed us of the cycle of trauma, of how the autonomic nervous system (consisting of the parasympathetic and sympathetic nervous systems) supports our survival, and of the intricate manner in which relationships can both cause injury and create repair. The contributions that PVT has made to the fields of neuroscience and psychotherapy are noteworthy.

Dr. Porges coined the term "neuroception," referenced earlier, to describe the way we automatically and involuntarily scan our environment, our own body, and interactions between people to discern whether or not we and they are safe.[10] Neurocepting is not something we think about doing—it is an unconscious, ongoing, and continuous process deeply connected to our survival. We are all neurocepting all the time—we're doing it right now. We don't have to think about doing it; our bodies just make it happen.

As long as our bodies detect no threat, we continue with business as usual—we can soulfully socially engage and be present in the world. It's when our bodies perceive threat that things shift and we change nervous system states. The autonomic nervous system shifts into the state necessary to handle the situation at hand. Social connection and intimacy are no longer the priority when a perceived threat is near.

Prior to PVT, we thought that we were immediately sent into a state of fight or flight when we perceived a threat. But PVT has informed us that something else happens first. We look to our community for support. When our neuroception tells us that a threat to our survival is present, which happens very quickly and via the soul nerve, our SES lights up. We automatically and rapidly show both on our face and in our body that we need help. Our facial expression changes, our pupils dilate, our body stiffens. If we were speaking, we may abruptly stop, or our voice may crack. This is so that if people are around who may help us, assuming their SESs are online, they will come help. We are literally wired to give and get help when in danger.

When there is no help around, either because there is in fact no one there or because the people who are present cannot or will not help us, this is when we move into fight or flight. This is the sympathetic nervous system (SNS) at play. If we are unable to fight or flee to safety, our bodies may freeze up in response. In an active freeze response, all the chemicals of the sympathetic system, like adrenaline and cortisol, are rushing through the body, but the body stiffens and tenses, with no ability to protect itself otherwise. The appeasement trauma response, characterized by a lack of consent accompanied by a lack of resistance (flight/fight), is an active freeze state. A prolonged active freeze state leads to a shutdown state (dorsal).

In shutdown, our bodies literally prepare for death. Our muscles go limp and we may actually collapse, or faint, if in the face of a physical threat. However, when the threat is more emotional, for example, a threat to our belonging, we may or may not go fully limp, but our bodies shut down all the same.

> *You remember Ocean from earlier. In childhood, when Ocean's father showed her love, each time only to violently take it away, the abuse was never physical, but her physiology reacted just as adversely. Emotional abuse is no less significant than physical abuse. Ocean's body would land in a dorsal, immobilized state as she was swallowed by a sea of shame. Shame is a shutdown state. It makes us want to collapse and hide. Shutdown is our body's last resort, as it's not a functional place to be long term.[11] This explains why we may unconsciously push the pain of trauma away. If we cannot stay embodied while connecting to the painful*

trauma memories, our nervous system (and ego) will work like mad to keep us away from this dorsal state.

MOBILIZING OUR PAIN

The SNS, responsible for the fight–flight–active freeze response, serves a useful function in our day-to-day, when all is well. Here the SNS supports harmony between the rhythm of our breath and the beating of our heart. In threatening situations, sympathetic reactivity is here for our survival—to move us quickly away from danger and toward safety. It's not ideal to maintain a sympathetic state, as it's too exhausting to stay so activated for long periods of time—it's not good for our physical or holistic health. Therefore, sympathetic's mobilizing energy is often moving us to another state. Deb Dana states that the goal of sympathetic is to mobilize us back up to ventral, as that is the safest, healthiest place to be long-term.[12] Sympathetic's role, then, by default, is also to keep us out of dorsal, as that is a biologically risky place to be.

To review, our social engagement system allows us to detect unconsciously and automatically if we are being met by another with warmth, care, love, and acceptance; or if we are being met with disapproval, rejection, or the potential for violence. When our bodies detect a threat to our survival, we go into an SNS response of fight, flight, or active freeze. Sometimes we land in a dorsal state of shutdown and collapse. And as dorsal is a biologically unsafe place to be, our SNS will try to mobilize us back up to ventral.[13] The surge of anger, the rush of rage, is actually our SNS trying to mobilize us from shutdown, a biologically unsafe place to be, back up to the safe haven of ventral.

When we are sent into a sympathetic state, there are several ways in which we may return to ventral, to safety. One way is that we can

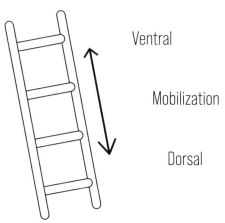

Figure 4.5 Autonomic ladder
Adapted from THE POLYVAGAL THEORY IN THERAPY:
ENGAGING THE RHYTHM OF REGULATION
by Deb Dana. Copyright © 2018 by Deb Dana. Used
by permission of W. W. Norton & Company, Inc.

self-regulate. We can use the internal resources we've acquired to get ourselves back into a calm, peaceful state. The other is that we can coregulate; we can be with a safe, regulated person who is in ventral, and that person's nervous system can help ours return to a place of peace and calm. Ventral begets ventral. This is the ripple effect of showing up grounded and compassionate out in the world.

Dr. Porges and Deb Dana call coregulation a biological imperative. It is a basic human need. As children, we need it to form a secure attachment and to later evolve spiritually. Even for those of us who have gathered the skills to safely self-regulate, we need love; we need community; we need a sense of belonging, validation, and care. We are literally wired for collective survival. And so, coregulation remains vital throughout the life span. On a spiritual level, we may sense that even our ancestors benefit from our capacity to coregulate with them, and we benefit from their capacity to do the same. When I dedicate the end of each chapter to the liberation of all beings, living and nonliving, it is with this understanding.

Immobilization is at trauma's core.[14] When we are left alone to deal with our pain, without opportunity for coregulation, trauma becomes lodged in our bodies. There is nowhere for it to go. This was Talia's experience in childhood, when she eventually shared her abuse with her mother, and her mother told her she didn't believe her. Talia collapsed, and all the pain, all the shame, all the rage had nowhere to move. Talia attempted to compensate, trying to make herself appear okay to the outside world. But deep within her was an inner child that held onto the burdens of unlovability, defectiveness, and shame, which Talia had been ignoring for decades. In learning to turn toward her pain rather than away from it, things began to shift for Talia. She was able to give to her inner child the compassion she never received from her mother or any of the core adults in her life. Bringing her pain to light, Talia and everyone in her life felt a profound shift. The grip of Talia's survival ego lightened, and day by day, she felt more like herself, more open, more free.

When sympathetic energy is unable to mobilize us back up to ventral, because we get no co- or self-regulation, we go into shutdown—dorsal territory. This is the space where shame resides. Shame is a direct consequence of rejection—of being told overtly or covertly that we don't belong. With coregulation comes a felt sense that we are accepted and loved for who we are, exactly as we are. Coregulation is healing. When we instead experience rejection from our community, whether that community is an individual person in our life, our family, a group to which we want to belong, or society as a whole, we collapse into a well of shame.

Deeply imprinted within our bodies is a survival need to be accepted by our people.[15]

When we are presented with a threat to our belonging, our bodies experience it first. Our bodies respond to rejection the same way they respond to a threat to our lives: The functioning of the organs below the diaphragm declines and our bodies literally prepare for death.[16] Acceptance by our community is perceived by our bodies as a life-or-death scenario because, if we are exiled from our community, our bodies believe that will be our inevitable end. So instead, we exile parts of ourselves. We abandon who we are becoming for the safety of fitting in. As children, particularly, there are no other feasible options. But fitting in does not equate with belonging. Fitting in is essentially shutting down who we are, shutting out our light.

Shutdown is far from freedom. Within the prison cell of immobilization we lose connection to who we are and find it impossible to express our truth. Such a life sentence restrains us in a holding cell where, though we may be alive, we're not really living. Dissatisfied with life, disconnected from a sense of worthiness, we live life behind a glass wall—we can see out but can't fully participate. It's actually biologically adaptive. If we can't participate fully, we're less likely to get kicked out of our community for doing something wrong, but we also miss out on the good in life, the satisfying relationships, the joy. If we're constantly worried that we may do something "bad," we can't be feeling really good about ourselves. We are constantly on the defensive; our rejection detector is working overtime. We'll do anything to stay an accepted member of our village, even if our behaviors show otherwise.

Shame is suffocating. It doesn't leave much room for self-compassion. We can't rush the parts of us holding the shame. These parts have burdens and stories to be witnessed. What we can do is turn up the light of bodhichitta and approach these vulnerable parts of us. We can bring embodiment to their immobilized way of being, help them feel seen, and self-liberate them.

✳

EMBODIMENT PRACTICE: BRINGING EMBODIMENT TO OUR SHUT-DOWN PARTS

Embodiment Preparation

In this section, we explore several yoga asanas (physical postures) to support the parts of us holding the trauma memory of immobilization. Yoga is a practice that supports embodiment. Yoga is a science, a philosophy, and a spiritual practice with South Asian roots, most specifically Indian. Yoga practice is estimated by scholars to be somewhere between 2,500 and 10,000 years old. As an ancient tradition that was first passed down orally, researchers debate when yoga was truly formalized, but what's clear is that this wisdom practice has been around for many centuries.

As an Eastern practice, yoga, like Buddhism, is a spiritual science that emphasizes returning to our true, awakened nature. "Yoga" is both a noun and a verb. It is a state of being, and it is an active pathway to achieving that state of being. We embark on yoga as a verb—the skillful, active path of awakening, until we access yoga as a noun—the state of awakening itself.

"Yoga" is a Sanskrit word that literally translates as "to yoke." But because words can lose some of their gusto when translated, the essence behind "yoga" is "to unify," "to join" or make one. Right away we see how yoga challenges the egoic notion of separateness. It challenges systems of oppression that are fueled by this false notion of separateness, and it offers a vehicle for resolving trauma and healing the sense of separateness that results.

Yoga is a practice of self-inquiry, a practice that helps us investigate our ways of being, bringing darkness to light, to evolve beyond our shadows and conditioning and achieve the state of freedom that is our true, inherent nature. When we quiet our minds enough to soften the ego and connect to our true nature, we find that we have always been free.

While parts of us may find a temporary sense of security in the dorsal state, this state is one characterized by disembodiment. This sequence of asanas (yoga postures) with breath is designed to help give your body what it needs when it goes into shutdown, but from an embodied space. We can teach our bodies over time that embodiment can feel safe.

We'll explore several forward-folding asanas as well as a twist. When trauma lands us in dorsal, the forward-hunched position is a space of disconnection and protection. With embodiment, we are shifting these poses from a space of disconnection and protection to one of introspection.

When trauma happens, we move to a space of immobilized stillness involuntarily, and accompanied by fear. The medicine in these asanas is that we are choosing to hold them—we have the freedom to choose immobility (and we can get up if parts of us don't like it), and we can do this without fear.

You will see that the following asanas have both mat options and chair options. You can choose to do this practice from a chair or a yoga mat. Note that if you choose a chair practice, wisdom posture and seated forward fold are identical.

If it feels accessible, practice ujjayi pranayama (see Appendix A) while in these yoga asanas.

EMBODIMENT PRACTICE

I invite us to begin by finding a comfortable seated position. Take a moment to consciously generate bodhichitta, a heart-centered intention to embody compassion and to be of service, to remove suffering within.

Ajna Chakra Asana: Wisdom Posture

Figure 4.6 Wisdom Posture in chair

Allow yourself to sit in a chair with your back supported (put a pillow or bolster between the chair and your back if desired). With your back supported, ground your feet to the earth. Put some yoga blocks or books underneath your feet if they don't easily touch the ground.

Sitting tall, take some deep breaths to connect your feet to the earth, to get present, and to invite in your spiritual supports, if it feels right.

When you're ready, let your chin nod down toward your chest, and roll your body forward until your chest is bending forward toward your thighs.

If your chest doesn't meet your thighs, bring some pillows in between them.

Find a comfortable position for your arms. If it feels right, you can let your arms extend toward the ground, bringing your fingertips toward some yoga blocks or books if needed.

If your awareness wanders away from your body, compassionately invite it back. Listen to what your body is asking for. *Move when the body needs you to move, and be curious about whether, eventually, stillness can feel safe.* If so, be still.

Take some deep breaths here or focus on the sensations you feel in your body.

Be here for at least 2 minutes if you can, and up to 5 or more minutes if it feels right, before mindfully exiting, returning to a seated position, and pausing to witness.

Figure 4.7 Wisdom Posture on floor

Floor Variation

You may like to lay a blanket down so that your knees have some cushion. Kneeling, allow your big toes to touch one another and your knees to be a comfortable distance apart. Your knees could hug a bolster if you would like (that's optional).

The ajna chakra is our third-eye center—our seat of intuition.

Sitting on your heels, invite your chest to lie forward over your thighs, your arms to extend forward, and your third-eye center (center of the forehead) to come to a pillow or the ground.

*Note: If your hips don't meet your heels, you may want to place a rolled-up blanket or bolster on top of your calves and see if your hips can come to rest on it.

Feel the parts of your body that are connected to the earth. Notice your body and witness your breath.

If your awareness wanders away from your body, compassionately invite it back. Listen to what your body is asking for. *Move when the body needs you to move, and be curious about whether, eventually, stillness can feel safe.* If so, be still.

Take some deep breaths here or focus on the sensations you feel in your body.

Be here for at least 3 minutes if you can, and up to 5 or more minutes if it feels right, before mindfully exiting, returning to a seated position, and pausing to witness.

Sukhasana: Comfortable Cross-Legged Seat

Figure 4.8

Allow yourself to come sit comfortably and pause to take several breaths before moving into the next asana/posture.

Paschimottanasana: Seated Forward Fold (Restorative Variation)

Figure 4.9

Roll up a blanket to place underneath your knees as you take a seat and extend your legs forward.

You could place your legs on a bolster or pillows here as well. If the lower back is feeling tight, stack up yoga blocks/books, a bolster, or some firm blankets to sit the hips on. Stack up as much cushioning as is necessary so that your body can rest as you bend forward, hinging at the hips.

You could lay your third eye down or turn your head to one side, moving your head to the other side when it feels right.

Allow your arms to extend forward and rest in this introspective posture.

Again, invite yourself to stay present. Consider sending compassion inward to whatever thoughts, emotions, or sensations arise.

Breathe and get curious about staying here for at least 3 minutes, or up to 8 minutes.

When it feels right, exit mindfully, sending gratitude, compassion, or affirmation inward, returning to a seated position, and pausing to witness.

Jathara Parivartanasana: Twist Posture

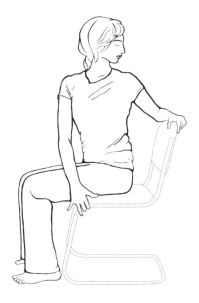

Figure 4.10 Chair variation

Allow yourself to come sit in a chair with your back supported (put a pillow or bolster between the chair and your back if desired). With your back supported, ground your feet to the earth. Put some yoga blocks or books underneath your feet if they don't easily touch the ground.

Sitting tall, take some deep breaths to connect your feet to the earth.

To twist, begin to slowly turn your body to the right.

Bring your left hand to the right side of the chair. If it feels okay, hook your right arm around the back of the chair.

Use your inhalation to lengthen your spine and your exhalation to gently revolve your body to the right a little bit more. *Listen to your body and try not to overdo it. Yoga is about embodied presence. You may feel sensation, but you should not feel pain.*

Breathe here on the first side for 1 minute, or up to 5 minutes, before coming back to center and pausing.

When you are ready, repeat on the second side.

When complete, return to center, breathe, notice, meditate.

Close out gracefully or move into the next posture.

Figure 4.11 Reclined twist on ground

Allow yourself to come lie on your back—bend your knees so that your feet are flat on the ground.

Allow your feet and your knees to touch each other. Reach your arms out long to either side of you (like a letter "T"). Keeping your feet where they are, lift your hips up and shift them left, placing them down on the left edge of your yoga mat.

Let your knees fall to the right. If your knees don't touch each other, feel free to hug a pillow with your knees, or place a pillow between your right knee and the ground.

Allow your head to look skyward or turn it to the left (find what feels supportive for you without strain).

Breathe here on the first side for 1 minute, or up to 5 minutes, before coming back to center and pausing.

Return to your starting position: knees bent, feet on the earth. Pause, notice, and breathe.

When you are ready, move to the second side.

When complete, return to center, breathe, notice, meditate.

Close out gracefully or move into the next posture.

Viparita Karani: Legs Up the Wall Posture

As an option, you might fold some firm blankets and stack them up against a wall.

Invite yourself to sit on the ground with your left hip up against the wall. If you have a pile of blankets, sit your left hip up on the blankets.

Spin to face the wall, lowering yourself onto your back as you do so, so that the backs of your hips are against the wall and your legs are going up the wall. You may need to scoot yourself a bit closer to the wall to get

Figure 4.12 Legs up the wall

your hips to touch. If using blankets, the backs of your hips are resting on the blanket here.

Invite your legs to relax if possible, bending your knees slightly, and breathe here.

Stay for as long as it feels right to you—about 2 minutes or up to 10 or more.

When it feels complete, exit by bending your knees into your chest and rolling to one side, gently lifting yourself up to a meditative seat to check in and breathe.

The chair variation is the same as the previous, aside from having the backs of your knees over a chair. Try to have the very backs of your knees, as opposed to your calves or ankles, over the chair so your hip flexors can relax.

Figure 4.13 Legs up the wall: Chair variation

Breathe and relax here for as long as feels right before rolling to one side and finding a meditative seat to breathe and check in.

CLOSING WITH INTENTION

I invite you to continue to visit the meditation practices from Chapters One through Three, and the asanas offered in this chapter, as well as the resources offered in the three appendices.

These practices are meant to be lifelong resources. Sending you affirmations and care for your willingness to remain open, to explore, to learn, and to evolve.

Tonglen Off the Cushion

I invite you to begin to use tonglen practice while off your mat or cushion. In your daily life, when you notice challenging emotions surfacing, I invite you to pause and imagine breathing those challenging emotions into your compassionate heart. Turn toward what you are experiencing. After several minutes, imagine breathing in the antidote to your pain, only after really giving the pain space to be acknowledged and honored.

Embrace the light and embrace the dark alike. Peace to you. Peace to all of us.

May the healing and benefits obtained by way of these words contribute to the liberation of all beings, living and nonliving, without exception.

5

BEFRIENDING WHAT AILS US

If you hope for more peace in the zworld,
you must begin by making yourself more peaceful.

—GESHE SONAM RINCHEN,
THE SIX PERFECTIONS[1]

L *ife brings suffering (and trauma).* There is a cause to that suffering. There is an end to the cause. The end arrives through the process of awakening itself. Early in the process of awakening, we can tap into our innate goodness and allow it to lead, our guiding light. Awakening continues as we cultivate the wisdom of emptiness (and equanimity) and turn up the light of our basic goodness into one of full bodhichitta (the awakened compassionate heart). Awakening cannot happen without bodhichitta. This means that suffering continues in the absence of compassion—and this includes self-compassion. Both wisdom and compassion are at the root of this journey.

Not all, but many, of the beautiful beings I've supported, over the past two decades as a trauma therapist and educator, had trouble tapping into their innate goodness. Something was blocking its access. Trauma, whether lived, generational, or systemic, has misinformed many of us about our worth, lovability, and belonging. Trauma, again, creates a separation inside that is mirrored back at us when we look outside. Based on what we've survived generationally, culturally, and within our families of origin (or adoptive family, or chosen family), we may have parts of ourselves that we really don't like, that we think are defective, or that we push away from our awareness.

The bodhisattva is someone who works toward yet delays their own awakening with the motivation to liberate all sentient beings from their suffering. Bodhichitta is born from the bodhisattva mission. Zen teacher Brother Chân Pháp Hải teaches that in the Sutra of the Eight Realizations of Great Beings, it's said, "The bodhisattva is one who makes the great vow to befriend all things—to befriend all beings." He says this is "not just beings outside of ourselves. It's developing the capacity to befriend all the different parts of ourselves."[2] This befriend-ing is inclusive and exhaustive. No parts of us are left behind. All is worthy of befriendment. Pháp Hải playfully calls bodhichitta "buddy-chitta . . . becoming a friend to everything and everyone."

The idea of making friends with all parts of ourselves may be off-putting. Many of us have parts we so desperately want to change, hide away, or fight into submission. It's important to remember a couple of the Buddha's key teachings here. First, impermanence: Nothing stays the same. This means even the parts of you that you dislike have the capacity to change and evolve. They are more than they appear to be at first glance.

Second, dependent origination: Nothing exists independently. This means that all parts of you exist based on the causes and conditions that preceded them. Feel free to turn back to the table example in Chapter Two for a refresher. The various parts of us are complex. As human beings, we are complex. Just as a stranger can know very little about us simply from a quick glance at our exterior, we cannot really know our parts until we get close to them and listen with an open heart.

So we need self-compassion on this journey of befriending the var-ious parts of us. Ironically, we likely have parts that make it hard to elicit self-compassion. Parts are manifestations of the ego, and the ego is an obstacle to self-compassion. Again, we don't need to villainize the ego or the parts of us that make self-compassion difficult. We've spo-ken about how healthy ego development is critical. If we have low self-esteem or difficulties with extending compassion, this is a sign that we need to nourish the sense of self before we can liberate it.

The practice at the end of this chapter allows us to do just that. I'll offer you the opportunity to consider, with love, which parts of you are blocking your freedom, which parts of you make self-compassion, or compassion in general, challenging. Perhaps there's a judgmental part, an intellectual or analyzer, an internal critic, or a problem solver inside that can't slow down long enough to extend love and care. I'll invite you to consider which parts of you attach or cling to ideas or ways of being; which parts carry aversion or hatred for other beings or other parts of you; and which parts create duality or see separateness, informed by the trauma they've survived.

✳

THE INTERNAL FAMILY SYSTEMS THERAPY MODEL

The internal family systems (IFS) model of somatic psychotherapy was developed by Dr. Richard Schwartz. While a Western model, developed by a Westerner, the Eastern and shamanic influences on IFS are undeniable, and Schwartz attests to this influence fairly often. To get to know the truth of who we really are, we must also get to know who we are not. This is what we do within IFS; we get to know the parts of us that ail us. There are many predecessors to IFS, the lojong teachings and tonglen practice being but one example. The Tibetan Buddhist practice of Chöd, established in Tibet by an 11th-century woman named Machig Labdrön, is a practice of intentionally going to the places inside that scare us, and feeding these parts of us to complete satisfaction, until they get everything they need from us—the end result is that our inner enemies transform into allies.[3]

A practice not dissimilar to IFS, called Feeding Your Demons, was established by one of my teachers, Lama Tsultrim Allione, as a variation on the ancient practice of Chöd, more accessible to the average Westerner. IFS offers another paradigm for the practice of turning toward that from which we typically run. IFS is not affiliated with any religious or spiritual tradition, but you will hear me reference Buddhist thought as we journey through an explanation of the model, because that is the lens through which I personally see IFS.

What's unique about IFS is the manner in which we connect to our own basic goodness and extend love and care to our parts. The level of emotional intimacy that can be cultivated between self and parts offers this beautiful form of internal attachment repair. When we didn't get what we needed as a child, we likely formed an insecure attachment with our caregiver. This impacted our healthy ego development and how we grew to relate to ourselves and others as adults. IFS offers a remedy of sorts, a way to be with each and every part of ourselves the way they needed someone to be back then. What we find is that our parts are so much more than they first appeared to be and that this innate goodness is actually within each of them.

Let's get into the nature of our parts here. In IFS we organize parts into three primary categories. We have our exiles. We have our managers. And we have our firefighters. I invite us to take a look at each of these three types of parts one at a time. As we do so, I invite you not to cling to these categories too tightly. As you get to know parts of yourself, you may be unsure if the part is a manager, a firefighter, or an exile—that's fine. To work with a part in the healing process, you don't have to know which category it falls into. Moreover, the categories themselves are not the embodiment practice. Knowing the categories is not what brings forth the healing.

The Buddha taught that fixating on certain aspects of life that offer nothing toward liberation is a misuse of time and space. Likewise, fixating on a part being a manager or a firefighter can be a distraction from working toward your own liberation. Knowing the category has nothing to do with the freedom attained when you work with a part and set it free. I only offer this information to give you a better idea of what you may be carrying in your own system. Take what resonates.

OUR EXILES

Our exiles are the parts of us that carry the deepest innermost expressions of the trauma we've survived—the pain, the vulnerability, the wounding, the consequential weight of oppression. If we experienced trauma as a child, these were the parts of us that remained present for the abuse or neglect. They are the parts of us that become highly burdened by negative thoughts, beliefs, and narratives about themselves. If we experience trauma reactions, such as flashbacks, nightmares, or intrusive thoughts, images, or sounds—it is our exiles that often hold these experiences.[4] If we tend to believe we're not enough, we're unlovable, we're alone, we don't matter, or we're defective, it's the exiles who grip these beliefs the tightest.

All parts of us manifest in the body. Exiles often show up as sensations, as tension, pain, strain, or discomfort in the body, oftentimes in our stomachs/guts, hearts, throats, or even our backs (though this varies for everyone).[5] As a side note, if we were to integrate understanding of exiles with Polyvagal Theory, we'd notice that exile energy is usually dorsal (shutdown/freeze with collapse), while remembering that our social engagement system is offline when dorsal energy takes precedence.

In IFS, we call the internal experiences carried by the exiles, burdens. Our exiles are typically frozen in time, stuck in the past when the emotional injury occurred. Because we exile them (usually without conscious awareness of doing so), they are left as small inner children to face the burdens of shame, guilt, rejection, abandonment, vulnerability, or humiliation from what they've survived, alone.

Our exiles long to be seen, heard, and loved and to have their pain and stories witnessed. They thirst for redemption. While they fear that whatever self-loathing belief they carry is their truth, they desperately seek someone to show them that they are wrong about themselves—that they are worthy, they are lovable, they do matter. Our exiles will often lead us toward relationships that are not good for us, looking outward for the redemption they desire.[6] Turning away from our own pain, we've gotten in the habit of looking toward other people to validate our worth. But now we are awake enough to know better. Now it is up to us to look inward to our exiles to help them heal. We are the only ones that can truly give our exiles the redemption they need. This is cultivating a healthy sense of self. This is the pathway to becoming free.

✳

During our first session, Imani (she/they) explained to me that she was forced to exile and stifle her queer identity, growing up in a religious community that both overtly and covertly invalidated her existence daily. Naturally, Imani's sense of self was injured as a child. Imani had learned to not only exile her queer identity but also her anger, because anger was not tolerated in her household. Imani had come out years ago, but she still found herself exiling parts of her sexual identity when she returned home to see family for the holidays. And she wanted to learn to love and validate her anger, to no longer push it down. When Imani began to befriend these parts of her and listen to their stories, these parts of her that she once feared became like dear friends that she honored and appreciated.

✳

Dejuan (he/him) experienced his parents arguing constantly throughout this childhood. He witnessed verbal and physical altercations and at times he described that he literally "became Dad's punching bag." A Black-Latinx man growing up in Brooklyn, Dejuan told me he wasn't allowed to be vulnerable in his home or community. Working with Dejuan, we found three young exiles whose vulnerability he had locked away many years ago, as there was no space for them. There was a 5-year-old who held the memories of the abuse; another young part, around age 6, who was depressed and held the beliefs "I'm alone. I don't matter"; and an angry 8-year-old who was met with denial, humiliation, and shame when he attempted to speak to his parents about their arguing when he was that age. In time, Dejuan was able to be with these parts and give them what they needed back then—the love and care that they hadn't received from his parents. Dejuan reported his body immediately feeling lighter at the very beginning of this work, and a year later he was out in the community helping young men in the prison system befriend their own exiled parts—learning to trust and love themselves.

To recap, exiles are the most vulnerable, pained parts of ourselves. They are often very young (taking on their burdens in early childhood). Common emotions or feeling states connected to exiles are shame, depression, hopelessness, helplessness, powerlessness, despair, inadequacy, worthlessness, loneliness, feelings of being abandoned and/or suffocated/claustrophobic, fear, and terror. Common exile beliefs are "I'm unlovable," "I'm broken," "I'm defective," "I'm different," "I'll never be able to do it," "I'll never have it," "No one cares about me," "I can't _____ [fill in the blank]," "I'm not good enough," "I'm alone," "I hate myself."

We also tend to exile parts of us that were unacceptable at home growing up. For example, if as a kid we were never allowed to experience anger (e.g., we would get in trouble or be taunted for being angry; "Wipe that silly frown off your face"), we then learned to exile our anger and likely continue to exile anger/rage (our own and others') as an adult. In this case, anger/rage would be an exile.

Our exiles are not only the parts that we excommunicate so as not to deal with their pain; they are also the parts that our families, communities, society, and culture tend to banish and marginalize. Those of us having marginalized identities have been exiled for our race, ethnicity, citizenship status, economic status, gender identity, sexuality, religion, body size, physical or intellectual ability, and level of education. This is what the term "marginalized" means—to be put on the margins. And so, as parts of us are exiled by society, the pain these parts carry gets exiled also. Sometimes we fall into the trap of exiling these same parts, as was Imani's experience. This is internalized oppression—we reenact inside ourselves the violent acts of the perpetrator/oppressive system on the outside.

The heavy pain of our exiles activates our protectors (managers and firefighters). Sometimes protective parts keep the exiles locked away for fear that the world will hurt them again. Other times, protective parts fear the exiles' pain will overwhelm us. Our internal systems work overtime to lock away the pain that our exiles hold, as to our bodies, it can often feel like we're going to die if we let the pain of our exiles surface. Other protectors may fear that we won't be able to participate in this high-demand world if we are in touch with the pain of our exiles. For example, if we are constantly connected to the shame we carry, we won't be able to function at work, because shame sends us into a nervous system state of shutdown—"collapse and disappear." Shame makes us want to run and hide. We can't function day to day if the core belief that we are unlovable is right there in our face. So our protectors push that belief down and lock it away.

Yet we are just as impacted by the banishment of our exiles as they are themselves. Try as our protective parts might to bully them into submission, our exiles will only remain silent and unseen for so long. When we hear people talk about being "triggered," what is happening is that the pain of their exiles has rushed into their conscious awareness. Darkness was brought to light in the most abrupt and disturbing way. Exiles are triggered to the surface constantly—the efforts of our protectors to keep them silenced are futile in the long term.

Our exiles are commonly referred to as "the shadow," the parts of us we keep in the dark or that we may not even be aware are there. Our protectors get very good at quarantining them out of our awareness. It's not uncommon that we'll need to work with many protectors first before they even let us access the vulnerable exiles they are hiding. Turning up the light of bodhichitta and befriending our exiles is often a courageous and necessary step in this healing journey.

The burdens our exiles carry are not their truth, even though it may feel like it to them. Exiles identify with their suffering. But we can help them heal. Our exiles need as much as any of us to know that they are not bad, that they are good, and that they belong. In IFS we say that, in their truth, our exiles are the most creative, spontaneous, playful, free-spirited parts of ourselves—they are beautiful parts to be celebrated. But until we help liberate them from the burdens they carry, they are forced into the painful role of inner outcast.

OUR PROTECTORS

In IFS we call our parts that are not exiles our protectors. Our protectors always have a positive intention, but their impact is usually far from that.

OUR MANAGERS

Our managers are the protective parts of us that have become fixated on controlling our internal and external worlds. They are very concerned with how we appear to others and are preoccupied with our acceptance and belonging. They are constantly monitoring how we feel and how others feel about us, as they try to keep any uncomfortable feelings at bay. They don't like our own discomfort, and many of them have a low tolerance for others' discomfort as well. Our managers are the parts that typically lead us through our day, so much so that many of us believe our manager parts are who we really are. We say, "I'm a perfectionist," "I'm a people pleaser," "I'm just logical."

Managers do just that—they attempt to manage our entire inner and outer life. They've come to believe there is no other way they can be. They have a sense of duty that this is what they must do. And they tend to believe that they are the only ones that can do it. For this they are often exhausted, or even resentful, because they believe they are "doing it all alone."[7] They, like our exiles, are often stuck in the past, believing we are much younger than we are. Like our exiles, our managers are often inner children themselves, yet unlike our exiles, they are the parentified children inside, attempting to perform a role they are not developmentally equipped to carry out.

Here are some examples of managers common to many of us: the "doer" or taskmaster; the perfectionist; the people pleaser; the caretaker that attends to everyone else's pain and neglects their own; the success-focused parts that are fixated on our financial gain, wealth, and/or power. The ones that focus on intellectualizing, analyzing, or explaining instead of feeling. The public appearance–focused parts that may manifest as the know-it-all, the one who is always right, the one who is preoccupied with our weight and physical appearance, the crash dieter, the obsessive-workout part, or the one who works over-time to make us look acceptable on paper.

Some of us have the self-victimizing part that generally sees them-selves as prey and denies a role in conflict; or the one that minimizes what we've been through in our past, the one that avoids confrontation, the peacemaker; or competitive parts with something to prove—the manipulative one, the serial dater, or the one who must one-up every-one because they are faster, smarter, more attractive, holier than thou, or better in some way. The list goes on, y'all.

Some of us have managers that control us by keeping us slightly dis-sociated all the time: the ones that stay high, stay just drunk enough to put a fog over our reality, or restricts our caloric intake so that we're always somewhat floaty and disembodied.

We all tend to have critical managers. We have the inner critics that ridicule, shame, and verbally assault us to keep us behaving, and the outer critics that practice various forms of bigotry and discrimination like racism, xenophobia, homophobia, transphobia, classism, sexism, misogyny, fatphobia, ageism, financial or educational elitism, and/or able-bodiedism.

These parts can feel like a handful, it's true. Especially since their voices often conflict with one another. You've probably tried to elimi-nate some of these from your system at various points, as this is often encouraged by our family, our peers, our society, and even some models of psychotherapy. The thing is, what we fight against becomes stronger. When we nourish that inside which needs care, it naturally transforms.

The most bigoted, hateful parts of people naturally shift when they are loved. The racist part of someone is protecting them from feeling their own shame, grasping at the one thing they feel keeps them lovable. When the parts they've exiled are loved and seen, the racist part no longer needs to behave in such a nasty way. In IFS we'll often ask a manager part if there is a job it would rather be doing, if that were an opportunity. When the part feels nourished and its fear is released, the inner critic would often rather be more like an inner coach; the people pleaser would rather be in charge of self-care; the racist and homophobic parts often really want to connect with people with different identities; the taskmaster wants to play; the food restricter wants to help with self-nourishment. Our managers long to return to the role that they were meant to have.

> *Imani found that her people-pleaser manager really longed to advocate for herself and others in her community. Dejuan learned that the part of him that code-switched really was a part that valued authenticity and wanted to help him and other young men of the global majority live into their authentic selves.*[8] *This is the profound impact of befriending the parts of ourselves that keep us from being free.*

OUR FIREFIGHTERS

Our systems will try just about anything to keep our exiles silenced. Most of our managers, like our exiles, are stuck in the past. Yet, because they are like parentified children, attempting to perform a job for which they are not fully equipped, there are going to be times when, despite all their might, managers simply can't keep the basement door closed. Times when our exiles get triggered to the surface. This is when our firefighters come rushing in.

When the pain of our exiles is triggered to the surface, against the will of our managers, it's our firefighters that rush in to put out the emotional flames. While our managers are preemptive and proactive, constantly planning to keep things just so, our firefighters are reactive. When they rush in, they are going to put out the flames, period! They are uncaring or unthoughtful about the repercussions. They don't care if we hurt ourselves and others in the process. Whereas managers are looking to keep us and sometimes everyone else comfortable, firefighters put the comfort of others aside and go!

Many of our firefighters are mobilized in fight–flight energy. We may have the ones who are vindictive; who lash out in rage; who vandalize; who physically, verbally, mentally, emotionally, spiritually, or sexually abuse others. We may have the ones that inflict self-harm—the ones who self-mutilate, who binge and purge, or who attempt to take their own lives. We may have the ones who thrill-seek as a reaction to pain, the ones who speed down the interstate at over 100 miles an hour when triggered, the ones that gamble recklessly, the ones who act out sexually on impulse, using sex as a way to objectify or feel powerful over others.

Other firefighters take us into a downregulated, collapsed nervous system state. We may have the one that wants to lie on the couch and binge-watch TV to escape their life, the dissociative part that makes us leave our body, the part that gets sleepy or falls asleep when faced with discomfort, the part that drinks or uses drugs to numb or escape, or the part that fantasizes about suicide.

Our managers, who try to keep us acceptable on paper, usually don't like our firefighters, because their behavior is shunned by our family and community. It's typically a manager that brings us to start therapy or pick up a healing journey, oftentimes due to the behavior of a firefighter inside.

Frankie (she/her) explained, "I have got to get out of this pattern" (this was a manager talking). "I give a presentation at work, and then this critical part of me just replays it over and over again, and it drives me crazy. So then I get out a bottle of wine [firefighter] and drink and drink until I'm so distanced from my anxiety that I can't do much but fall asleep. But if I do stay awake, then I just feel incredibly depressed and worthless. I'll text my ex, and he'll just ignore me. Then I just feel more worthless. I've got to stop drinking." While drinking wasn't helping Frankie, it was a reactive behavior to a deeper issue—feelings of low self-worth and inadequacy that were actually rooted in childhood. Frankie's drinking firefighter took the heat, but this part was actually trying to help her escape some real pain underneath.

Firefighters take a lot of heat. In their attempts to put out fires, they usually create them. Our managers tend to dislike our firefighters, and our firefighters tend to dislike one another. When I invite clients to "go inside" (as you would in a meditation) and be with a firefighter part, it's common that they'll first hear all these other voices reacting to the behavior of the firefighter. For example, when Frankie first attempted to go inside and befriend her drinking firefighter, she was met with many competing thoughts coming from other parts like, "This behavior has to stop!" "You shouldn't drink your pain away!" "You're nothing but a drunk." "Don't put all your business out there. Don't let them know about this."

Our families, communities, and society punish the behaviors of our firefighters. Too much firefighter behavior will land you in rehab, the psychiatric hospital, the homeless shelter, or prison. As a society, we are scared of firefighter behavior. And it's understandable—their behavior is irrational and impulsive. And they are also trying to save us—just not going about it very well.

Both firefighters and managers often take on their roles at the same time that our exiles are burdened—at the time that the pain, the rejection, or the trauma happened. The roles firefighters took were necessary for our survival back then, but firefighters, like our other parts, don't realize that the trauma isn't still happening—that they can change their behavior because we are now away from danger.

And when it comes to systemic trauma, which is ongoing, meaning we are never really safe from the danger of it—there is no aftermath. Systems need to be fully dismantled for lasting safety to be felt. However, we still benefit from helping our parts heal by liberating them beyond the role they've gotten stuck with. We do have agency over our own suffering to an incredible degree. If we are an activist, when we work with our own parts we can show up for our activism embodied, awakening, and free, and be of far more benefit than if we are only focusing outward on the systems of oppression. We take for granted sometimes the ways that we oppress ourselves—leaving parts of ourselves abandoned and alone.

THE HEALING AGENT WITHIN

In IFS, the term "Self" is used to describe the one inside who is not a part. This Self is resilient, undamaged by trauma, and innate to each of us. It is wise, curious, unbiased, calm, grounded, and compassionate. In "polyvagal speak," it has the ability to maintain the ventral state, and so we could say it has the ability both to self-regulate and to help our parts with this internal form of coregulation. This Self is essentially the healer within, and it can help all of our parts heal and evolve.

Self is not dissimilar to Buddha Nature—it's our innate goodness.

Yet, because Self is active inside the system, I liken it even more to relative bodhichitta—our awakened, compassionate heart that motivates us to alleviate suffering, both inside and out in the world. Given that in Buddhism we see shortcomings in emphasis and exaltation of the Self, I'm replacing "Self" with "bodhichitta." It's the radical compassion of bodhichitta that can heal the hurt parts of us. Quite accidentally, I've come to use the term "Buddhism-informed IFS" (BI-IFS) to describe this slightly different take on Self as compared to traditional IFS.

I do want to point out that in IFS there is no hierarchy between Self and parts. It's not parts "bad," and Self "good." Yet and still, given our ego and our conditioning, which leads us to categorize and hierarchize things by default, I find that thinking of Self as the healer within, particularly as we spell it with a capital S, can easily mislead us into exalting Self and devaluing parts. I have also witnessed, at times, the tendency to fixate or cling to this idea of Self and parts as separate entities, reinforcing this idea of separateness.

In the Buddhist framework, we would describe parts as the ones who carry our afflictions, defilements, and ego tendencies. And from this perspective we would also consider all parts to be empty, meaning all parts are equal. Emptiness, again, is the merging of space and awareness, and it is the nature of all things. All things are empty of solidity (impermanent), and empty of independent origination. Engaging with the IFS model through a Buddhist lens, I've come to note the equanimity and nondual nature of self and all of our parts. Extending bodhichitta to our parts, as opposed to locating Self as the inner healer, is what I offer here in BI-IFS.

There is no need to exalt some parts of us and demonize others. This is our ego tendency, but it is also a cause for our suffering. We can see parts for what they are: empty. Empty is not a negative thing; it's a liberative thing. It's not saying our parts don't matter; it's saying that each is as worthy in its own regard as much as any or all things can be worthy. This understanding of emptiness (ultimate bodhichitta) allows for the relative bodhichitta of compassion to be poured into our parts. Many of our parts have been waiting for us for so long, they desperately need this compassion. So in the BI-IFS meditation that follows, I will be inviting us to generate bodhichitta, rather than to connect to Self as it would be done in traditional IFS. May the practice be of benefit.

✳

EMBODIMENT PRACTICE: BEFRIENDING A PART

Embodiment Preparation

The next meditation is a compassion practice that will invite you to befriend a part of you that you typically turn away from. You can also use this meditation to revisit a part of you that you have befriended in the past. A friend checks back in, so even when we've befriended a part, we want to revisit it regularly to see if it needs our support or care.

If you'd like to draw or write during this practice, I will offer places for you to pause and do that. Feel free to grab some paper and any utensils to draw or record with if that resonates.

This meditation does not need to go smoothly the first time. There are two ways to go about it.

1. No agenda: Connect with your body and be with what is most present (the part of you that's most present will reveal itself through physical sensations, emotions, thoughts, or even images, colors, etc.).

or

2. You can choose a part to befriend today. Perhaps create a list of parts you may be interested in working with (e.g., the inner

critic, the intellectual, the conflict-avoidant one, the angry one, the perfectionist, the smoker, the "past is in the past" part). Then decide which part you would like to befriend today. Optionally, you could choose to draw an image or symbol that represents this part of you or write a bit about it.

Note that just because you decide you want to work with a particular part today doesn't mean this will be the part that's most present when you close your eyes and go inside. Compassion involves working with the part that is suffering the most at the time. If it becomes clear that another part of you needs your attention, be with that part instead and come back to the other one later.

Beginner's Mind and Bodhichitta

We all tend to have managers that are intellectuals—they pride themselves on being logical, and often, their mantra is "I know." They know it all already (they believe). When I work with clients and they identify a target part (a part of themselves, as it's manifesting in the form of a body sensation or maybe a belief), it's not uncommon that clients will say, "I know how this part got here," or "I know why this part does this." When this happens, it's usually the client's intellectual part talking. We really want to approach our parts from a space of open-hearted compassion. "I know" gets in the way of us truly getting to know a part's side of the story—"I know" is a refusal to listen.

Beginner's mind is about relaxing what we think we know and instead adopting the mindset that we simply don't know. Uniting beginner's mind with bodhichitta, awakened compassion shown inward, we can be with a part and truly see it, hear it, get to know it, even validate it, nourish it, give it what it needs. So as we move into this embodiment practice, I invite you to notice and have grace for the parts of you that expect, anticipate, and know. It is of service to acknowledge these parts and invite them to relax, to notice if they're willing, and stay curious if they are not. Turn up the light of awakened compassion as you move in, shining light into spaces once dark.

> Please use the practices in the appendices if and when needed.

EMBODIMENT PRACTICE

Begin to turn your attention toward your body. If it feels safe to do so, close your eyes or lower your gaze. Feel free to consciously connect your feet or seat to the earth, and/or call in any of your spiritual resources.

I invite us to consciously generate bodhichitta—a heart-centered intention to embody compassion and to be of service, to remove suffering within.

If you have an idea of what part you'd like to work with, think about it and see where you start to feel sensation in your body. Otherwise, begin to notice sensations in your body (even numbness counts as sensation). *Where in your body do you land?* (If it's "everywhere," that's okay too). Stay there for a bit with a mindful focus.

Breathe.

How would you describe what you feel in your body? (e.g., "A whirling in my head," "A heaviness through my entire body," "It feels like it's to the right side of me, talking at me.")

Take plenty of time to notice each of the following; pause and notice after each question. . .

Is there a texture there?

Is there a shape?

Is the sensation active or still?

Is it speaking? Is it loud or quiet?

What size is it?

If you stay focused on it, do you begin to notice anything about it that you didn't notice at first?

✳

If you notice any resistance (a little or a lot) to this practice (e.g., a part that's overthinking it; a part that's critical of you; a part that's fearful of doing this type of work; a part that wants to hurry up and help the little child), acknowledge it, validate it, and invite it to relax. If it relaxes, keep going as you were. If it won't relax, start the meditation from the beginning with this new part (locating it in or around your body, etc.).

If there is no resistance at all and you're feeling open, curious, calm, compassionate, or loving toward this part, let it know how you feel toward it (speak the words silently, directing them within). Stay with the part and notice what's happening.

(If at any point during the meditation, resistance of any kind appears, acknowledge it and invite it to relax, and if it won't, begin the meditation over again, befriending the resistant part.)

If this is feeling like enough, pause here and go to Closing Out on page 137.

If you're wanting to go a bit further, let's keep going.

✳

<u>*What are you noticing about the part now? Is it open toward you? Trusting?*</u>

<u>If not</u>, keep a gentle focus on it while staying curious as to what it may need from you to be more open or trusting in time.

<u>If so,</u> you might ask this part if there is anything it needs you to know about it. Listen inward with patience and compassion. Notice.

If you sense a response from this part, validate it. (E.g., "I get that you are trying to keep me in line. You don't want me to be embarrassed at work," or "I hear you. You want me to perform well," or "I see. You got this from Granddad.")

Are you beginning to get more of an understanding of this part? Can you acknowledge its pain and the story it's been carrying?

<u>*You might ask the part, "How did you get here?" or "What created you?"*</u>
Pause and listen inward for a response.

Is there anything you sense this part wants you to know about its experience? Or is there anything it needs you to witness? (For example, if it's a part that other parts don't like, such as a substance-using part, it may need you to hear how hard it's been to be vilified in the system. Or if this part was alone when something adverse happened, it may need you to witness it along with it—allow this part to share with you what was so hard about the experience, for example, "I didn't have anyone to talk to about it, and it was so scary. It confused me and made me think there was something wrong with me.") Be sure to validate the part and let it know you hear how hard it was for it.

You could ask the part how old it is, and/or how old it thinks you are. Listen and validate.

If the part thinks you're much younger than you are, you can update it—imagine showing it what your life has been like during the years it's missed.

If the part feels like a "doer" (manager or firefighter), you could ask the part what it's afraid would happen if it didn't do what it does or say what it says. (E.g., if it's the critic, "What would happen if you didn't berate me all the time?") If you sense a response, listen and validate.

If it feels right, you might ask, if it didn't have to do the job it's doing, what would it rather do? (E.g., if it's the critic, "If you didn't have to shame me all the time, what would you rather be doing?" "If you weren't always so worried about saving me from embarrassment, is there something else you'd rather be doing?")

Continue to validate the part, care for it, and offer it hope.

※

CLOSING OUT

First, offer gratitude to the part of you you're currently working with. Let this part know it has a relationship with you now, and you'll continue getting to know it. See if it has anything else it needs to share with you before you close.

Second, see if this part has a way it wants to stay connected with you between now and the next time you return to this practice (some parts will want you to check in with them regularly).

Next, send gratitude to all of your other parts—both the ones you met today and the ones you've yet to meet. Send a loving message of gratitude inward. Send the message inward that you will return.

Feel your feet against the earth. Offer your presence to the earth—perhaps gratitude to the earth and any spiritual resources you've been working with. Take your time to mindfully exit this practice.

Optional: Journal about your part(s) and meditation experience; draw an image that represents your parts/experience, or use art, creative expression, music, or dance to illustrate your experience.

Additional Embodiment Practice: Tonglen With Parts
Practice tonglen meditation with a part: Inhale and imagine taking away the pain from this part of you; exhale and imagine sending this part the antidote to its pain.

CLOSING WITH INTENTION

How are you feeling? What's on your heart? What does your body need?

Parts work can be joyful. It may feel like a breakthrough one day and messy and overwhelming on another. All of it is welcome. All of it is impermanent and a part of the path.

If you happened to tap into the pain of an exile today, honor how you're doing. Many people find working with their managers and firefighters more manageable, but appreciate the support of a licensed therapist to do the deeper exile work. Honor what your system is telling you. Receive help if necessary.

Some people find the first time they do something like this that they are met with a cacophony of overwhelming voices coming from different parts inside. This too is normal. If you begin to adopt a regular practice of going inside to be with your parts, they'll get the message that you'll be returning often, and they'll bombard you less when you go inside. When some clients get overwhelmed by too many parts speaking at once, I invite them to pause, breathe, and repeat this affirmation inside: *"I hear you. I see you. I know you need me. I'm coming."*

Return to this and the other practices in this book regularly. Parts usually need more than one visit to be witnessed and to feel free.

After the meditation, I invite you to stay curious about which parts of you are showing up in your day-to-day. Do you have a body ache one day? Return to this practice. Did your skin break out? Return to this practice. Inflammation in the body? Intense moods from out of the blue? Ruminating thoughts? Return to this practice. Our parts lurk underneath each body sensation, feeling/mood, or attitude.

I invite you to honor yourself and acknowledge your courage, simply for showing up to do the work. The work is not always easy.

I invite you to rest. I invite you to breathe. I invite you to do something restorative for yourself.

I invite you to stay curious about it all. Find lightheartedness when and where you can.

Laugh, where it's possible. Find joy in this process.

✳

May the healing and benefits obtained by way of these words contribute to the liberation of all beings, living and nonliving, without exception.

6

TRANSFORMING THE LEGACY

Healing Generational Trauma

If you look deeply into the palm of your hand, you will see your parents and all generations of your ancestors. All of them are alive in this moment. Each is present in your body. You are the continuation of each of these people.

—THICH NHAT HANH, *PRESENT MOMENT WONDERFUL MOMENT: MINDFULNESS VERSES FOR DAILY LIVING*[1]

*M*any of us connect to the knowledge that we have the opportunity to heal in ways that perhaps our ancestors didn't. That
we are the dream our ancestors envisioned. If it feels right, I invite
you to dedicate this part of your journey to your ancestors, including
the ancestors of the land you are on. Call in their spirit if it resonates.
Let's begin.

OUR ANCESTRAL INHERITANCE

Our ancestors knew in their bones, in their guts, at their core, that
the blood carries data. Before the days of neuroscience, the scientific
method, and evidence-based protocol, our people held the truth within
their bodies—a deep sense of inner knowing that the body's wisdom
and pain alike are carried across generational lines. So what I am about
to share with you is not new, modern-day scientific genius. It's prehis-
toric, ancient wisdom, as old as time, and transmitted to us through
intuitive understanding and ancestral connection.

When we connect to our bodies and learn to regulate our systems
so that we can get quiet within, then we can finally hear the intuitive
messaging that resides there. When we access a physical sensation
in the body, there is often an image that goes with it, an emotion, a
message, a memory. And oftentimes, these memories are beyond what
we have directly experienced; they are ancestral—relating to a transgenerational pattern that has become imprinted and passed along to
us from our parents, our grandparents, our great-grandparents, our
ancestors as a collective. The ancestral burdens and the ancestral

heirlooms alike are held in the body. As we approach the pain, we also approach the gifts.

The scientific field of epigenetics, while potent and interesting, is in its infancy in comparison to the ancestral intelligence we can access when we create the space inside to do so. Our Indigenous ancestors knew this. And while we will explore the science here, I offer that we also hold in our hearts the full understanding that what we read in a book in no way outperforms, in validity or value, our direct lived and inherited experiences. The intuitive avenue and the logical road are not distant strangers; they are the closest of kin. If we follow their related paths, we often land on the same understanding.

ANCESTRAL TRAUMA AND EPIGENETICS

Epigenetics is a field gaining ever-growing interest in the mainstream. Epigenetic research shows that we inherit the experiences of our ancestors via our DNA. When we experience something stressful, for example, the expression of our DNA is altered to reflect that stressful experience, and those altered stress genes are passed down to our offspring. Genes are malleable and impressionable in a positive way as well.[1] When we heal, gene expression is transformed in a beneficial way, and these evolutionary heirlooms are also passed down to future generations. When we take the time and energy to heal ourselves with intention, we are transforming the legacy and offering a more peaceful and connected existence for our children and the generations to come.

When a birthing person is 5 months pregnant, if they are carrying a fetus that will be assigned female at birth, this fetus already has a fully formed uterus and, within that uterus, all 7 million eggs they will need to one day carry and birth their own babies. This means that at 5 months pregnant, we are not carrying only our own child; as Mark Wolynn, author of *It Didn't Start With You*, writes:

In your earliest biological form, as an unfertilized egg, you already share a cellular environment with your mother and grandmother. When your grandmother was five months pregnant with your mother, the precursor cell of the egg you developed from was already present in your mother's ovaries.[2]

We shared an internal environment with our grandmother and mother when we were a fetus in our caregiver's womb. But what about our patrilineal line? The findings are parallel. Wolynn shares that when your father was a fetus in his mother's womb, the precursor cells of the sperm you grew from were already present. This means a piece of you was present within your grandmother's body when she was pregnant with either of your parents.

We experience what our parents experienced in some way, whether through biological, intergenerational passage or through that which we picked up from them socially. Our nervous systems are incredibly vulnerable to what is going on around us. How our parents, other children and adults, and society as a whole relate to us after we are born and throughout our development will impact how we receive and pass down stress and joy alike in a sociobiological way.

How does this look socially? If our caregiver/parent never developed a healthy sense of self, perhaps they were led at times by the various parts of them holding pain and trauma. Just as we have parts, our parents have parts. We pick up these behaviors as children and mimic them, developing our own correlating parts, and sometimes the behavior of these parts begins to look like our personality. In polyvagal language, if our parent was often in dorsal (shutdown) or fight-or-flight modes, these are both scenarios where the social engagement system (SES) is offline and where we cannot effectively attune or extend love and compassion to our children.

A parent in shutdown may experience their upset, crying child and look blank or unresponsive. The child's SES interprets this as a threat—"No one can help me"—and if this happens often enough, the child's system will default to dorsal as well, collapsed and disengaged, knowing their needs cannot be met by their environment.

When it's society as a whole that conveys overtly and/or covertly that we are the "other," we compensate for the sake of our own survival, and these ways of compensating are passed down both genetically and generationally by way of living in a social climate that sustains the message that we are other. For folx belonging to identities that are marginalized, the people pleaser, the perfectionist, the code-switcher, and the anxious part are often partly related to the necessity of surviving in a society that criminalizes us for traits beyond our control.

PERCEPTION MAKES IT TRAUMA

When I facilitate trainings in the Trauma-Conscious Yoga Method, I emphasize that perception is what makes something traumatic. I'm not referring to perception on a cerebral front, since you remember from our polyvagal chat that it is our bodies that perceive threat, via the soul nerve. Two different bodies could be in the exact same situation, and one could perceive the situation as threatening and the other could perceive the situation as unthreatening. Our history, both lived and inherited, stored in our bodies, informs our nervous system reactivity, which determines whether or not our bodies detect threat. Our perception is unique based on our lived experience as well as the trauma responses we've inherited.

In the last several decades, cell biologist Bruce Lipton has conducted research on the prenatal ecosystem that speaks to the importance of perception in relationship to what is passed down to offspring. Lipton's data shows how perception informs our genetic inheritance. Lipton's research validates our ancestors' intuitive knowing—perceptions are passed transgenerationally from parent to offspring.[3] Let's note that perception is not fact and is rooted in bias. The Buddha noted that attachment, aversion, and delusion are the seeds of suffering. Biases are perhaps the root of delusion and inform our attachment to some (people and things) and aversion to others. Biases of all kinds are stored in our bodies. They become our wiring (karmic inheritance); they can lead to our disembodiment, and they inform our nervous system's reactivity and threat perception.

We all carry biases. We carry biases that are explicit—accessible by our conscious awareness—but many if not most of the biases we hold are implicitly encoded in our brains and bodies; we are unconscious of the fact that they even exist within us. This is essentially the premise of Resmaa Menakem's pivotal work, *My Grandmother's Hands: Racialized Trauma and the Pathway to Mending Our Hearts and Bodies*, which speaks to the reasons why Westerners have tried, yet failed, to eradicate systemic racism and white body supremacy.

We have focused on the cerebral and on thinking or talking our way out of racism, but racism and racial bias are not cerebral; they are nervous system reactivity that is held in the body. Why are so many unarmed Black folx regularly murdered by the police? Menakem explains that blue bodies (that is, police bodies) have received the same racial conditioning we all have here in the West, and their nervous systems respond to Black bodies as threatening, whether or not they are armed. This is the harmful power of bias. It has the capacity to spread like wildfire through an entire collective—the refusal to see clearly, which informs the bias, is also that which upholds it.

If we look back at Polyvagal Theory and neuroception, we're reminded that we are continuously and unconsciously scanning our environment to determine whether a threat to our survival is present. The only way a fetus has to understand if there is a threat to their existence is through

147

the childbearing person's chemistry.[4] Lipton found that a pregnant person's perception of their environment informs their chemistry and thought fields. Their environmental impressions are carried to their offspring by way of their blood. This data-rich blood crosses the placenta, which allows the fetus to decode the childbearing person's chemistry.[5]

The fetus is able to interpret the emotional experience of the childbearing person through the blood, and this too becomes the fetus's biology in utero.[6] When a childbearing person is joyful, the fetus is joyful. When a childbearing person feels fear, the fetus feels fear. When the childbearing person holds a bias, the fetus, too, takes in that bias, and the eggs or sperm already present within that fetus are encoded with that bias as well. This is perhaps the root of how racist ideology and racial bias, for example, have managed to sustain themselves for centuries—they are literally being handed down through the generations genetically. There is also a sociocultural passing around of racist ideas, which we'll get to in just a moment.

Dr. Rachel Yehuda, director of Traumatic Stress Studies at Mount Sinai School of Medicine, states that "epigenetic changes biologically prepare us to cope with the traumas that our parents experienced."[7] Our biology has no context for time or place, but, born with the same set of tools as our parents, our bodies believe we'll be able to survive. Yehuda coined the term "environmental resilience" to refer to this generational passage. The emotions and perceptions of the childbearing person change the genetic programming of the fetus so that the fetus is more likely to survive in the same environment following birth. And again, it's not only the fetus inside of the childbearing person's body that is impacted; the eggs or sperm of the developing fetus (the third generation) are also altered.

Our body is well intentioned in passing down the altered stress genes along the generations. The challenge is that we are not truly living in the times of our great-great-grandparents. We are trying to collectively overcome our sense of separateness and division. But we've inherited these neurobiological responses to threats that are different from the ones our grandparents lived through. Those of us doing the "othering" (all of us) and those of us who are "othered" (all of us), are responding to a neurological default mode that keeps us from being free. Even bringing consciousness to this is awakening. And with intentional generational healing, the capacity to evolve is all the more possible.

THE POWER OF IMAGERY TO HEAL AND TO HARM

Images are powerful, and they create a biological, psychospiritual, and emotional imprint within us. A strikingly beautiful image will stop you in your tracks—and a gruesome or violent image will do the same. Images alone are so powerful that, if they are violent, by themselves they can create trauma in our systems. Images are deeply embedded in our bodies and unconscious, individually and collectively. Images have the power to do great harm. They also have the power to heal.

Many forms of meditation use imagery as a tool for support, embodiment, transcendence, the cultivation of greater peace within. Imagery and visualization are used in many forms of psychotherapy because it's been found that positive imagery can change our neural wiring and serve as a powerful resource to create new patterns of embodiment and behavior.[8] The IFS meditation from Chapter Five often brings up intuitive imagery as we connect with the various parts of ourselves.

Both mental imagery and physical art can serve as transformative vehicles. If we rehearse in our heads the visualization of a loving caregiver, attending to us as children with all the qualities of an ideal parent, including unconditional love, nurturance, and protection, even if that wasn't what we really got in childhood, our brains change and our bodies, psyches, and souls feel the positive shift from this envisioning.[9]

Imagery makes a lasting impression in our bodies, minds, and hearts. Images can evoke love, and they can just as easily elicit fear. The media, oppressive systems, and people in power use imagery frequently to uphold a status quo, knowing our minds are so wildly susceptible. Images make a big impact on how our bodies perceive the environment. Images, when used manipulatively, can train us to fear, hate, and "other" one another.

We were talking about perception earlier and how it's rooted in bias, which is held in our bodies. We pass down our perceptions and conditioned biases generationally. So what is the relationship between imagery and generational trauma? Between imagery and karma (cellular memory held in the body–mind)? When imagery is consistent and repetitive, but it's negative, how does that affect our biases and perception, and how is that passed along?

When it comes to white supremacy culture, we have all been encoded with implicit and explicit messages, informed by racialized trauma (racism), that then inform collective perception and manifest to this day as unresolved collective trauma that binds all of us—keeping freedom and collective joy just out of arm's reach. For example, throughout our history, we have seen people of the Afrikan diaspora depicted as slaves, as criminals, as prisoners, as subhuman, as animalistic, and so forth, over and over again. These images have been intentionally paired with narratives that empower their implicit imprinting, with the goal of sustaining a system of white body supremacy.

The system of white body supremacy and anti-Blackness established itself on the false declaration that Black folx were subhuman, dangerous, dumb, savage, and requiring control by force. Imagery was a primary means for conveying this untruth. Our minds are vulnerable, very vulnerable. When we see something repeatedly, we begin to believe it. And these beliefs are transgenerational.

Ava Duvernay's documentary *13th: From Slave to Criminal With One Amendment* exposes that the Thirteenth Amendment, which abolished slavery, contained an intentional loophole that excepted criminality.[10] The film reveals the ways in which this loophole was systemically exploited and used as intentional ammunition to uphold new forms of enslaving, immobilizing, controlling, binding, imprisoning, and murdering people in Black bodies in "the land of the free."

In *13th*, several of the interviewees refer to a 1915 film called *Birth of a Nation*, which was used as a means to aggressively beat into the collective conscious and unconscious alike this contrived idea that Black men were sexual savages and a threat to the safety of white women everywhere. And if Black men were a threat to white women, they were obviously a threat to white men—and that's what this film was really getting at. It sought to elicit increased violence and rage from white folx, particularly white men, toward Black folx in a society that already hated them.

The film depicted Black men (who were actually white men in "blackface") not only as a threat to white women's sexual safety but as being justifiably murdered by KKK members. The film and its propaganda helped confirm within the white consciousness of the time that Black people, particularly Black men, were subhuman, barbaric, and needing a superior, more Godly race to oversee them. Now, truthfully, it was white men who had been legally raping enslaved Black women for hundreds of years, but the film conveniently left that out.

Scholar, writer, and activist Ibram X. Kendi, in his book *Stamped From the Beginning: The Definitive History of Racist Ideas in America*, writes:

> It became almost standard operating procedure to justify klan terrorism by maintaining that southern white supremacy was necessary to defend the purity of white women. Black women's bodies, in contrast, were regarded as a training ground

for white men, or a stabilizing "safety valve" for white men's "sexual energies" that allowed the veneration of the asexual pureness of white womanhood to continue.[11]

We see how the cis-hetero-patriarchy and white supremacy have worked hand in hand for centuries—objectifying all Black bodies while concurrently objectifying, yet elevating, the white female body to the status of trophy as a means to further empower cis-hetero white male superiority. There are countless historical and present-day examples of imagery being used as a force for harm, and to review even a decent sample of them is beyond the scope of this book. I include enough here to get you thinking, and perhaps to get parts of you activated.

Pause. Breathe. What's happening in your body? Let's not ignore what we are feeling right now. *What inside needs you?* Lean into the discomfort with compassion. Discomfort is the gateway.

We don't have to pass down the same maladies that have been handed down to us. Being with the suffering within shifts our gene expression, and we pass down the heirlooms without passing down the burdens.

ANCESTRAL TRAUMA: LEGACY IN THE BODY

In this chapter I'll be offering several embodiment practices to you, and for this first one, I invite us to go ahead and dive in rather than wait until the end.

As we approach this practice, I invite us to refer to the passages we just read about the legacy of anti-Black racism in Western society. Please reread the passage if needed to note the body sensations, thoughts, feelings, and images that arise for you when you think about racism, homophobia, or any particular type of injustice. The way you experience this practice may feel different when you refer to a particular injustice that particularly marginalizes you (based on race, religion, sexuality, gender identity, etc.) versus one where you are given privilege.

After rereading the aforementioned passage, or thinking about another area of injustice if you choose, I invite you to turn to Chapter Five and go into the Embodiment Practice: Befriending a Part, working with what you are currently feeling in your body–mind.

Once you've closed your practice, I invite you to return to this page to continue forward.

LEGACY BURDENS

In Chapter Five, on internal family systems therapy (IFS), we began to talk about burdens. Burdens are the deep wounds carried by our exiles that we unconsciously or consciously push out of our awareness for our survival. Our protectors, the managers and firefighters, may carry burdens as well. Oftentimes, the protective behavior exhibited by a manager or firefighter is, in and of itself, a burden for that part.

A burden is feeling like we have to do something. Or it can manifest as a compulsive or impulsive way of being. For example, the binge-drinking firefighter who picks up a bottle of wine every time a twinge of loneliness arises (the loneliness likely belongs to an exile) has a compulsive way of being. The loneliness is the exile's burden, but the compulsive drinking behavior is likely a burden to the drinking part, particularly if after the binge-drinking episode there are feelings of guilt (I did something bad) and shame (I am bad).

It's often a combination of beliefs, feeling states, and somatic presentations that create a single burden. The burden of loneliness, for example, may come with a "pit in the stomach" and the narrative, "I'm different," "Nobody cares about me." The burdens we carry may be personal, meaning we picked them up by way of our direct lived experience. But many burdens are what we call legacy burdens in IFS. These are the burdens we've inherited socially and culturally by way of our unresolved, collective, historical, and generational trauma.

Legacy burdens include what we picked up from our families of origin, and they also include ongoing societal problems like racism, white body supremacy, the patriarchy, ableism, nationalism, and the like—the harmful attitudes and biases we've collectively adopted, consciously and unconsciously. A legacy burden of racism is experienced differently by somebody in a Black or Brown body versus someone in a white body, but none of us bypass the internalization of this legacy burden to some degree. Racial legacy burdens often manifest as denial by the dominant culture, who collectively deny that white supremacy culture exists and that racism is even a problem. The denial that slavery was "that bad" and that Native peoples of this land were violently massacred and displaced is a disembodied denial and repression that is commonplace and which limits all of our freedom.

All systemic trauma—that is, trauma that is built into the very infrastructure of our society by way of laws, policies, and regulations that elevate people in some bodies while oppressing people in other bodies— is ancestral in nature. The oppressive systems that have been put in place by wealthy people in power have sustained themselves through the generations. The more we consider each of our parts and their behavior or the roles they take within our internal system, we may begin to recognize that so much of what we are carrying doesn't even belong to us—it's the leftover residue of generations past.

✳

EMBODIMENT PRACTICE: WHAT'S MINE AND WHAT'S NOT

Embodiment Preparation

As you begin acknowledging your parts, befriending them, and getting to know their various ways of being, it may have crossed your awareness at times that your parent or sibling or grandparent or another family member also struggles with a similar thing. Say you have a part that is conflict avoidant, and you recognize that your mother and sister do too. You think back further, and you understand that your mother actually got this from her mother, your grandmother. And perhaps your grandmother got this from her parents, who grew up in a time when speaking in their own voice would have gotten them killed. This conflict-avoidant part is holding a legacy burden—an intergenerational trauma response that's sustained itself through the lineage. Next up, I'm going to offer you a little something different—a contemplative practice that will invite you to consider which of your burdens don't fully belong to you—which of them are actually the pain of your ancestors, or stem from cultural conditioning, as opposed to your own stuff.

✳

I invite you to begin by finding a comfortable position for your body. You could even revisit any of the meditation or asana practices in this book prior to beginning this exercise.

At the least, I offer that you begin by generating bodhichitta—a heart-centered intention to embody compassion and to be of service, to remove suffering within and out in the world.

Part 1: What's Mine and What's Not

If you haven't done so yet, take some time to write out or record some of the various parts of you that you're recognizing within your internal system (e.g., the workaholic, the critic, the binge TV watcher, the "push it down" part, the minimizer, the perfectionist).

Choose one part at a time and go through the following questions:

- What are some primary characteristics or burdens this part is carrying?
  - (Here's an example with Niko [they/them].) Niko wrote down that they have a perfectionist part. Some burdens/ traits this part carries are: 1. Anxiety. 2. The belief, "I'm a fraud. They are going to find out. I have to do this right." 3. It's exhausted. In befriending the part via the meditation practice, Niko learned that this part has little fuel left; it's been doing this for so long.
  - Your turn: Write down some of your chosen part's ways of being, thinking, and behaving and/or its burdens.
- What belongs to me?
  - Take a breath and reread what you wrote in response to the previous question. Then connect to your body and breath and notice what physical sensations are present. As you connect to this in your body, ask yourself, *What percentage of this pain belongs to me?* (Note the first number that comes to mind without thinking too hard—this tells you how much of this burden is personal and how much is legacy.)
    - (Here's an example with Niko again.) Thinking about the perfectionist part, they connected with it in their body, noticing a deep rumbling in their low abdomen

and a tightness in their chest. Niko asked themselves what of this belongs to them, and the first number that came to mind was 5%—meaning only 5% of this burden comes by way of Niko's lived experience; 95% is legacy.

Choose another part and repeat the above questions. Do this for as many parts as you like now, knowing you can always return here later.

Before moving to Part 2, take a look at all of your responses to the last question above. Take a moment to pause and reflect: *How much of this stuff really belongs to me?*

It's likely that some of it is yours (it's a consequence of your direct lived experience) but that much of it is actually not yours (it's ancestral).

What does that mean for you? What does that bring up for you? (Journal/reflect.)

Part 2: The Lives of My Ancestors

- What adversities did my ancestors have to go through?
  - How did the impact of these adversities manifest as burdens for my ancestors?
  - What of this may I have inherited?

Take your time and write as much as you can.

- In what ways did my ancestors perpetuate harm on a social level?
- (*For example:* Did your ancestors exhibit racist ideas, did they own slaves, did they speak derogatorily about queer or trans folx, did they enforce ableism?)
- In what ways did my ancestors perpetuate harm on an individual level?

- (*For example:* Do you have an ancestor who was physically, sexually, or emotionally abusive? How did the impact of abuse impact the family line?)
- Do I have a negative or positive outlook toward my ancestors? Is there room for repair there?
- (*For example:* Am I tempted to disown any of my ancestors for their behavior? When we do this, we are disowning some of the pain we've inherited, which doesn't heal the intergenerational impact. Even this is something to turn toward and heal. Get curious about repairing your relationship with your ancestors who did harm, knowing those who suffer on the inside pass that suffering around to others—knowing people are more than their harmful, hurt parts.)
- What are some of the burdened ways of being I've adopted to feel safe based on the areas in which my identity is "othered"? (E.g., because of my race, ethnicity, skin color, socioeconomic background, biological sex, gender identity, or sexual identity. *For example:* perfectionist and people-pleaser burdens are often at least some percentage legacy.)
- Did I leave anything out? Are there any burdened ways of being not mentioned yet that I've possibly inherited from my ancestors?

When you look back over all of this, reviewing your responses, do so with as much compassion as you can muster. These questions are meant to help you wake up and become more free, not as fuel for self-disparagement. Use what you've awoken to as material to work with in the Befriending a Part practice, as well as the embodiment practice at the end of this chapter.

✳

MAINTAINING HOPE: LOOKING FOR THE LIGHT

The COVID-19 global pandemic brought on new and unprecedented waves of grief and trauma that we were not collectively prepared for. The high levels of fear and uncertainty were an inevitable response to "the gap"—what we refer to as the bardo in Tibetan Buddhism. We visited the gap, the bardo, in Chapter Two, and I invite us to revisit it here. The gap is that transitional space, sometimes uncomfortable, other times terrifying, from which all can surface—pain can arise, and so can opportunity.

With the pandemic shift, many of us had to locate new ways of satisfying our sense of purpose. We had to get creative around how to maintain our work and our play. The move to working from home and, for some of us, spending twice as much time at a screen has been and still is taxing for a lot of folx. All types of parts get activated for us parents, attempting to work at home while homeschooling our children. But with this collective shift, something powerful happened—a new surge of care and concern about the unjust taking of Black lives at the hands of the police.

Could it be because we were collectively grieving and seeking meaning and purpose, in the depths of a collective spiritual crisis, that such a shift could occur? Or because we were on our devices so much more that the painful truth we could once turn a blind eye to we could no longer ignore? Perhaps because lots of us had more spaciousness in our schedules at the beginning of the pandemic, we had room to be more awake to what was truly happening around us. Collective pain can be an impetus for collective action. Pain can bring an opportunity to expand consciousness.

With the murder of George Floyd, shortly after the senseless killing of Breonna Taylor, more conscious, collective action was brought to the seeking of justice for Black lives than we had seen since the civil rights movement.

While the backlash against justice seekers was indicative of the bigoted status quo mentality, many of us simultaneously saw glimmers of light and hope, while mourning the absence of righteous action for decades past. There are still many who protest against social progress, their exhausted manager parts no doubt leading them toward an early grave from the stress of resisting change. But progress doesn't stop just because there are those who protest it. The world keeps going. The karmic cycle continues.

In Chapter Four, on Polyvagal Theory, we spoke about how immobilization is a biologically dysfunctional place to be. We can stay shut down for only so long. The same goes for our society. We can stay shut down for only so long. As for the United States, we can deny the truth of colonialism, of the mass genocide of Native Americans, of the horrors of the transatlantic slave trade, and of the continued perpetration of anti-Blackness and white body supremacy for only so long. While it may appear that the surge of care and concern has fizzled out, I stay focused, and I stay optimistic. Change comes in waves. Resistance to progress will not stop progress in the end. I choose to stay on the path, to stay present, to stay driven, to awaken. Stay with me.

Embodiment Preparation

The following embodiment practice is inspired by the IFS method for healing legacy burdens and by the work of IFS trainer Tamala Floyd. Gratitude for these teachings and teachers.

For the following embodiment practice, choose one legacy burden (can manifest as an emotion, belief, pain, etc.) you'd like to work with today. This can be something from your family line, or it can be something that is more cultural.

As a note, in IFS, each legacy burden is considered to be held by a part of us. You can identify the burden and know that it's being carried by a part of you. You don't have to know anything else about the part, other than that it's holding this burden.

✳

EMBODIMENT PRACTICE: HEALING ANCESTRAL TRAUMA

I invite you to find a comfortable position for your body. Connect your feet to the earth and take several breaths. Call in any spiritual resources you work with if that resonates. If it feels right, close your eyes.

I offer that we begin by generating bodhichitta—a heart-centered intention to embody compassion and to be of service, to remove suffering within and out in the world.

<u>*Choose one legacy burden*</u>.

Once you've identified the burden you're going to work with, take some time to acknowledge how this burden has presented itself in your life throughout the years.

How has it protected you?

How has it kept you from being free?

Take your time here.

Send compassion to the part of you carrying this burden, if you are able. If you're not able to hold some level of compassion or curiosity for this part, you may want to work with the part of you that is resistant to this using the Befriending a Part meditation from Chapter Five.

Begin to connect to the part/burden in your body. Where in or around your body do you sense it?

What physical sensations go with it? Pause, be aware, and breathe.

Is there any part(s) of you that fears releasing this legacy burden? (Do you feel any resistance such as an inner voice, a physical sensation, a belief or a feeling that informs you of resistance toward releasing it?)

If so, please don't rush your parts. Return to the Befriending a Part practice in Chapter Five to give any resistant parts time to be with their fears. Offer compassion and understanding to this part. Relax any parts of you that are critical of this part.

When all parts of you are ready to release this burden (e.g., you feel no resistance inside in the form of thoughts, feelings, and body sensations), think about a place in nature you'd like to go to release it. Imagine yourself there.

Think about all the living relatives who also carry this legacy burden. Invite those living relatives to join you in this place in nature—envision them there with you. (Note: If any of the living relatives are people you find unsafe, you don't have to invite them to your nature place. You can imagine them receiving the healing from afar. You could also choose to invite them but keep them separate and contained in some way.)

Next, think about all the ancestors (deceased), the ones you know and the ones you don't know, who carry this legacy burden. Invite them to this nature place as well—envision them there with you. (Note: Same as before, if you feel unsafe with any of these ancestors, see the options listed above. *Also,* you do not have to know what your ancestors looked like—they can be represented by any image, symbol, energy, feeling, essence, or sound.)

Invite all the living relatives, all the ancestors, and yourself to form a circle. Envision this.

Think of the earliest ancestor who does not carry this legacy burden. *(It is okay if you have to go all the way back to the earliest ancestor to ever exist in your lineage. You can imagine what they looked like.)*

Allow this well ancestor to stand at the center of your circle. Pause and take as many deep breaths as you'd like just to be here.

When it feels right, again acknowledge where you hold this legacy burden in your body. Imagine it releasing out of your body. Imagine it releasing out of the bodies of all those in the circle. Imagine the well ancestor in the middle, taking the legacy burden (they will not have to keep it— they are just taking it for now).

Let this process last as long as it needs to. *Notice your body. Breathe.*

When the legacy burden has been released from the bodies of all those in the circle, *envision the well ancestor in the middle, giving the burden back to one of the elements* (earth, water, fire, air, light, space).

Pause and notice. How are you doing? How are those in the circle doing?

Do you notice any discomfort in your body or mind? If so, you can always go back and repeat this practice again, locating the legacy burden in your body and sending it out.

If discomfort persists, return to the Befriending a Part practice in Chapter Five, befriending this discomfort.

✳

Next, think about all the beautiful qualities, the ancestral heirlooms and gifts, that your ancestors possessed. Allow the well ancestor at the circle's center to extend these qualities, heirlooms, and gifts to all in the circle.

Imagine receiving these gifts in your body. Take your time. *Breathe. Notice.*

When that feels complete, imagine all of these heirlooms being passed forward to the future generations. Take your time.

How are you doing? How is your family doing?

Celebrate. Envision your people celebrating and connecting, if it feels right.

Soak up any positive feelings this practice has brought you, and when you're ready to come out, do so consciously. Take time to journal/record, move your body, or be in a meditative space of self-inquiry or self-care.

Follow-Up

- In your day-to-day life, continue to check in with the members of your circle. You can do this by remembering this meditative experience, creating art, or returning to a meditative state to reconnect with them. Sometimes going through this practice once is all you need. Other times, it takes being in this practice multiple times to experience the shifts in an embodied way. As needed, repeat this practice in the future, with the same legacy burden.

- You can also repeat this practice with any of the legacy burdens you identified.

- In your day-to-day, notice any shifts for your parts—notice the ways you show up or respond to various situations or people differently. Stay curious about the impact of this work.

- If you were unable to make it through the practice and found yourself returning to the Befriending a Part practice, that is normal. Oftentimes a part or parts of us are not ready to let go of the legacy burden for reasons of loyalty, fear of loss of connection to the ancestors, or a host of other reasons. You can't rush your healing. Practice patience with yourself and return to these practices often.

Additional Embodiment Practice: Tonglen for Ancestors

Practice tonglen meditation: Inhale and imagine taking the pain away from your ancestor(s); exhale and imagine sending your ancestor(s) the antidote to their pain. This can be done with one ancestor or a collective of ancestors, and you do not have to know what they looked like.

✳

CLOSING WITH INTENTION

At this point I've shared a significant amount of information and insight, as informed by various cultural and spiritual belief systems and my own personal practice. I've offered a variety of meditative practices that build on and align with one another. And I've invited you to consider the impact of your lived and inherited conditioning.

Compassion for self and others has been an emphasis along this journey. I invite you to take some time to see what is present for you now. What parts of you are you feeling called to explore more deeply? What parts of you are you wanting to change immediately or avoid altogether?

How is compassion evolving for you? Bring it all onto the path. Be gentle with yourself, and I'll see you in our final chapter.

May the healing and benefits obtained by way of these words contribute to the liberation of all beings, living and nonliving, without exception.

7

SEVERING OUR
ATTACHMENT TO SUFFERING

Suffering is a choice that we're making. I can't keep identifying with the suffering because it's the suffering that depletes me. Identify with the space. Our natural state is not a state of contraction.

—LAMA ROD OWENS[1]

We need to realize that each of us holds the key to our own freedom. . . . You are the gatekeeper to your own happiness. No one can give us the answer. It all begins at home.

—REV. ANGEL KYODO WILLIAMS,
BEING BLACK[2]

WHAT YOU SEE IS WHAT YOU GET

The way we wake up, the way we become free, is by coming to know the nature of our own body–mind. This includes befriending all parts of ourselves and all parts of others. It involves staying curious and compassionate and remaining mindful of shunyata, the empty nature of self and all phenomena. In Buddhist psychology, external phenomena are understood as a mirror, reflecting back at us the state of our own body–mind. Waking up and becoming more free involves awakening to the faulty ways in which we may perceive things, while compassionately holding the knowing that, in its natural state, our mind is already awake.

If we haven't yet befriended and supported the parts of us that block self-compassion, it will be far too easy to trash talk ourselves as we come to examine our own biases and faulty perceptions. This is why I save this for our final chapter. If we are currently establishing a healthy sense of self or working on self-compassion, I believe it best to focus on befriending the many parts of us—the ones that blame and the ones that carry shame. If our critic is loud, it will be extra tempted to berate us in this next part of the practice. The message from me to you is, take your time before moving forward. Befriending our parts is a lifelong process. If the practice of befriending is new, it deserves lots of attention. We all have many parts, and they could all use our care.

The Buddhadharma (teachings) supports us in healing trauma and retraining the body–mind to see what is really in front of us, as opposed to that which is the appearance of our own trauma reflected back at us. Yet self-compassion is critical in this process. So invite that to be your area of focus first, if needed. When it feels like you can approach this next section while holding some level of compassion for self, then I invite you to meet me here. No need to rush your process. Perhaps the part of you that wants to rush through could use some befriending. And, when you are ready, let's continue.

When we look out into the world, what we see reflected back at us is the contents of our own mind. If we have an exile holding a negative core belief such as, "I'm unlovable," as we look out into the world we will find evidence for our unlovability. If a part of us has internalized the belief "people are bad," we will find evidence for this belief everywhere. Likewise, when we believe people are good or that we are, we find evidence to corroborate that. What we look for, we see. And this is unconscious to us. This is why befriending all the many pained parts of us that make up our ego is crucial to our awakening and freedom.

When we don't do this, we get stuck. We get stuck in our anger, or self-loathing. Prior to and early in our healing journeys, we make others responsible for our pain. Now, I'm not saying you are responsible for your trauma. I am saying we are each responsible for how we respond to ourselves in response to the trauma we've survived. And it doesn't even have to be trauma that makes us point the finger—it can be less severe than that. Think about a time you recently felt activated (triggered). How did you respond? Early in our journey, we look outward and point the finger when we've been activated. We think, "You did this to me," "You made me feel this way." It's true people do and say some messed-up things. But in reality, no one outside of you can activate you. The activation, the nervous system rush, the response from your parts, is coming from within you. We activate ourselves.

We are activated because what the person said or did struck a chord with us. A part of us believed them. Our ego detected a threat to its survival. Our inner world was mirrored back to us, and perhaps we had been pushing things down for a long time and weren't ready to look in the mirror but, "Bam, there it is!" When someone says something negative to us, it bothers us, because on some level we believe them. And sometimes we don't have to wait for anyone to say anything directly. We perceive someone to be suggesting we're stupid because we believe we are. We sense someone is about to attack our character because there's an exile in there carrying deep shame and our hypervigilant manager is ready to protect us against feeling that shame.

In Buddhadharma, we are invited to extend gratitude to the people we perceive as pushing our buttons—these folx are walking us along the path to Buddhahood. They are raising a mirror and giving us something to work with. In IFS, Dick Schwartz refers to these folx as our tormentors. If we choose to perceive them differently, they're actually our mentors, showing us exactly what we have left to work on—introducing us to the parts of us that need our friendship and care.

When I am infuriated with someone's behavior, if I choose to go inside and look within, I find several things. I find parts that are heartbroken and hurt. But I also find a part of me that has the capacity to behave as horribly as the person I'm infuriated with—a part of me that I don't want to look at. But when I choose to cradle and welcome that part into my heart, it has the opportunity to become something loving and beautiful. We can take responsibility for our stuff and offer it space and care. We can turn inward instead of pointing the finger outward, and our lives will be happier and more peaceful for it.

We don't see external phenomena for what they are; we perceive them based on our history, biases, and conditioning. I invite us to look at nirvana and samsara as an example.

As external phenomena, in Eastern wisdom traditions like Buddhism, Hinduism, and yoga, samsara is the cycle of birth, life, death, and rebirth, which we continue to navigate until we become awakened. "Samsara" also refers to the world of material existence. It's the world we live in, the world to which the bodhisattva vows to return, despite their attainment of awakening, to help all beings get free.

Nirvana, on the other hand, is the space of the awakened—it is enlightenment. While nirvana and samsara can be viewed as external worlds, more so, they are states of our own mind. As it's succinctly delivered within the commentary of Chogye Trichen Rinpoche's sacred text *Parting From the Four Attachments*: "Nirvana and samsara are both rooted in the mind." Samsara is a metaphor for the mind-made suffering. Yet, as the text illuminates, at the heart of the Buddhist Lamdre teachings from which the text draws is the "inseparability of samsara and nirvana":

> There is no abandoning of samsara in order to achieve nirvana, as the mind is the root of both. Once mind is understood to be the root of both, it follows that nirvana is just a transformation of samsara.[3]

How we perceive the world is dependent on us. When our trauma leads to perceptions that create separation, we have a choice to heal and see things in a more liberative way. To some degree, samsara is a choice we are making. Choosing nirvana is synonymous with bringing our pain onto the path, looking inward as opposed to outward—choosing to allow the unpleasant, even shitty, occurrences within our lives to serve as material for our awakening. As Jérôme Edou writes in *Machig Labdrön and the Foundations of Chöd*, "All phenomena are not other than mind and mind is not other than Buddhahood."[4] If we can choose to identify with our own Buddha Nature (space, awareness, clarity) more and more, and if we can befriend the parts of us that keep that wakeful nature beyond arm's reach, we can choose nirvana. Why not choose to wake up?

﹡

We perceive what we see to be real, accurate, and true. We see something, and we say it's real "because I saw it." The eye is what gives us sight. But when the eye sees something, it simply sees it—the eye alone cannot come to name what it is. The mind, informed by the body, does that. The eye itself cannot name what it sees; it can only see. It's the body–mind working with the eye that informs us of what we see. Two people from two different cultures may see very different things while looking at the same object.

When we see something, hear something, or smell something, we don't just take information into the body–mind and stop there. Given the sight, sound, or smell, we have a full-on sensory experience, and this information, by way of the soul nerve, travels from our body to our brain. Our mind interprets it using self as a reference point. We say, "Mmmm, that smells good to me," or "Ewwww, I don't like that," or "Why the fuck are they looking at me like that?!" We can't really make ourselves stop doing that. But what we can do is become aware of what's happening.

We can have a flash of awareness. We can observe, "I'm having an experience right now, and it's informed by the various causes and conditions that landed me here at this moment. Is my response helpful? Is there a better way?" We can recall emptiness—all things are equal—there need not be a strong attachment or aversion. We can call in the parts of us that hold the strong attachment or aversion and see what they need.

The Buddha taught that suffering is not pain; suffering is an aversion to pain. We choose suffering when we fight against the reality that pain and pleasure are simply different sides of the same coin. Life will bring pleasure and it will bring pain. The third noble truth, there is an end to the cause of our suffering, speaks to how a choice to relate to life differently frees us up to truly live.

TRUST IN YOUR OWN INNATE GOODNESS

I want to be explicit: I am not saying that we should not trust our bodies or our guts. Quite the contrary. We want to be with what is arising within the body, in a mindful, caring way. We want to listen to our bodies, understanding that the body holds both the trauma memory and the wisdom needed to heal and transform that memory. So hold that wisdom of truth in your heart that your body already knows everything it needs to know to heal and to be free. It's more that when we are activated or upset by life, we can turn inward and be with what is hurting. Knowing our mind is already awake, wise, and compassionate, when we experience struggle inside, we know there is healing that can be offered. But what if parts of us have gotten really comfortable in samsara and aren't interested in nirvana?

WE ARE MORE THAN THE TRAUMA WE'VE SURVIVED

Sometimes parts of us don't want this to be nirvana. Sometimes we get comfortable in samsara. At times parts of us have been in pain for so long, they are afraid to give that pain up, for without this pain, who will they be? Our true nature is boundless. It can be experienced, but it cannot be pinpointed, and it cannot be identified with words. It cannot be categorized. Yet our ego needs to attach itself to something, so oftentimes, we start to identify with our suffering. Even when we identify with our pain and our trauma, a contracted state, the ego will cling.

We start to oppress ourselves, placing ourselves in tight boxes that don't allow for the true expansiveness of our being. We say, "This pain is mine," "This is who I am." Our body–mind is very susceptible to the implicit and explicit messages it's met with. Entire systems of oppression have preyed on this fact. When we tell ourselves something over and over again, we create new neural pathways in our brain that align with the message, and we encode that information into our bodies. We begin to own what we've decided, or what somebody else has told us, is our truth.

Yes, the ego over identifies with the body–mind's experience. Yet this is to be expected in the aftermath of trauma. When something traumatic happens, it happens to "me." "I was assaulted." "I was injured." "I was scared for my life." "I didn't get what I needed." "There was no one there to love me." All of this is very real for us. How we feel having survived something unbearable is to be respected. We need to be listened to, seen, and validated. During trauma, it is our ego and our nervous system that save us. The parts of us that were able to fight back, or the parts of us that needed to disappear and play small to survive, all of these parts need validation and compassion. Being with ourselves in a loving way opens the door for releasing our identification with the trauma we've survived.

When we believe something is "mine," and we repeat that belief over and over in our heads, our brain believes it—we become wired for it. And if something is mine and something happens to what is mine, I suffer. I will fight to keep what is "mine," even when what I'm fighting for is suffering itself. So we cling to our suffering as though it's our true identity.

When new clients come to me for somatic psychotherapy, it's common that they will say something along the lines of, "I don't know who I am." They are searching for something solid that they can pinpoint and say, "This is me. This is my self." The idea that spaciousness is perhaps our nature can sound too groundless, too overwhelming in the beginning. We spoke about the bardo being that ground of expansiveness and possibility. It's the space in between—a chapter has closed, but another has yet to be opened.

While full of potential and possibility, this can be a frightening place. This is the place people are often in when they begin therapy. Again, we are in the bardo all the time. All things are impermanent; something is always ending, something else beginning. Yet we fight against this place. We want certainty. So we cling to our pain at times. And at others we attach to the eight worldly winds.

THE EIGHT WORLDLY WINDS

The Buddha taught of the eight worldly winds as a way to describe how we cling to samsara (suffering). Fueled by either attachment or aversion, in samsara we navigate these eight worldly concerns. They are the attachment to pleasure and the aversion to pain, the attachment to gain (success) and the aversion to loss (failure), the attachment to praise and the aversion to blame, and the attachment to significance/fame (a need to "be something") and the aversion to insignificance.

If the eight worldly winds are what inform our existence, we will be blown away. Their measurement and qualification are subjective and, given the way the ego works, their attainment will never be enough. When the ego gains something pleasurable, it wants to hold onto it forever. Gain doesn't bring happiness or peace, because we become preoccupied with trying to keep what we've got while also gaining more. The entire system of white supremacy was built to support the gain of people in white bodies at the sacrifice of people in Black and Brown bodies. Yet, as we see, people in power are not free. They are in constant fear of losing their power.

As all things are impermanent and dependent on the causes and conditions that preceded them, a life fixated on the eight worldly winds is a life characterized by deep dissatisfaction. Notice in these eight there is nothing relational. None of them have much to do with love, intimacy, or connection with others. At times we might use other people to achieve gain, pleasure, a sense of significance, and praise, but that is different than true intimacy and connection. And this behavior points to a calling inward—the parts of us that behave in this way need our love and care.

This need to "be something" is what hooks many of us. We've internalized faulty messages about who we are, and we believe we are not enough. When people come to therapy, this is oftentimes some of what they are unpacking. We think we want to "be better," "be more," "be something else," when in fact we just want to feel differently. We want to feel happy; we want to feel free. The void we feel inside is a lack of healthy sense of self—our inner exiles carrying burdens of shame and despair.

We think what we want is external to us. When we realize that the eight worldly winds will not bring lasting nirvana and recognize that what we've truly been searching for is love and belonging, that in and of itself can be liberative. This was my experience when I began examining the ways in which the eight worldly winds appeared in my life. Seeing it on paper was eye-opening. "How much of this really matters?" I thought. What matters to me is love, heart-centered service, compassion, community, and connection. That, to me, is nirvana. What is nirvana for you?

FREEDOM IS RIGHT THERE ON THE OTHER SIDE

My two-year-old daughter and I had just returned home from a walk. We came in through the garage and then opened up the side door to our backyard to go check on our dog. Having left the side door open, when we came back into the garage we saw a beautiful dragonfly. It seemed to be in a state of desperation, frantically trying to get out of the garage by flying into the door's window again and again. It couldn't get free. It kept trying the same thing over and over again, though it just wasn't working. "If only it could just see that all it has to do is fly several inches left to exit out the door," I thought. It kept trying to fly through the small crack between the door and the wall instead.

I tried to help usher it out, but it was too scared of me. As I looked at the dragonfly struggling, I noticed how much we as human beings are like that. We keep trying and trying the same thing that isn't working, clueless that freedom is right there on the other side of the door. As I became distraught, my daughter became enthusiastically distraught (she is a toddler, y'all). Gazing at her sweet little face of concern, I realized I was trying the same thing too, and it wasn't working. I decided to open the door further, hoping I wouldn't squish the dragonfly. And once I did that, my daughter and I walked out the door, and the dragonfly followed. Perhaps sometimes we need an example too.

SEEING CLEARLY

When we come to understand that what is right in front of our eyes is actually our own mind, our awareness grows. We can change how we see by changing our own internal ecosystem. When I decide, "This is nirvana," I am choosing now. I am choosing this moment. I am not looking for any other moment to be better or more than this one. I've long resonated with these words, by Rolf Gates:

> When the Buddha touched the earth he was saying, "I choose now. I will not give the power of this moment away to the past or to the future. I choose now. I do not need more time, or less time, or another time. I choose now. I do not need to be

more or to be less; I choose the person I am. I choose now. I do not need the golden age, an age of reason, or the romantic period. I choose now. It is enough for me to have this body, this breath, this moment. I choose now. I have the power to choose this moment, and when I use that power this moment becomes the moment I remember who I am. Each time I touch the earth this moment becomes the moment I awaken."[5]

LET'S NOT GET CARRIED AWAY

The Buddha taught that clinging is a root cause of our suffering. He even advised against clinging to his teachings too tightly. The teachings are merely a raft to get us to the other side. Once we get to the other side, we no longer need the raft. The wise lojong teachings talk about the shunyata trap—what is sometimes called "the poison of shunyata." If you take this idea of emptiness too far, it becomes poison.

My teacher Lopön Chandra Easton explains that emptiness is not to be viewed as an object, but rather a quality. She says, "It's a quality of reality like wetness is a quality of water."[6] Shunyata is to be a form of protection. The wisdom of the empty (spacious, awake) nature of all things offers a source of refuge. Yet, if we cling too tightly to this teaching, if we take emptiness too literally, or if we view it as an object, then we think, "Nothing matters anyway. Everything is empty." This form of nihilism is characterized by carelessness—a lack of fully participating in the world. It's a sort of "What's the point?" mentality that doesn't necessarily ease our suffering.

This is why the wisdom of emptiness needs compassion to enliven it. Compassion is a deep caring. Everything matters. All beings matter, yet they are all equal. They simply don't appear that way to our mind that's forgotten its awakened nature. But if everything matters, then won't we care too much?

The wisdom of emptiness offers an experience of equanimity, and we need equanimity to make compassion possible. Equanimity is having neither an attachment to nor an aversion to anything. It's an allowance for what is to *be*. It's an acceptance. Look inward and outward to help alleviate suffering, but also know that we have no control over the choices anyone else makes about removing their own suffering. We can only be responsible for transforming our own experience into nirvana. The bodhisattva will not force someone to change or wake up (it's not possible), but they will always hold the door open for them, knowing that one day, when they are ready, they may walk through.

Sometimes wisdom and compassion look like creating boundaries; sometimes their union looks like releasing our agenda to control outcomes and other people. Each of us will wake up in our own time. When it comes to any of the teachings inside and outside this book, my invitation to you is to always take what serves you and release what doesn't. Try not to cling to any of it. In truth, the answers lie in you. There is no teacher that can swim you across the sea of darkness to the shore of light. The guru is within.

TAKE GOOD CARE OF YOUR OPEN HEART

The bodhisattva promise to remain awake in the world for the sake of all beings is a noble one. Awakening is not always easy. Awakening does not discriminate. When we wake up to the light, we also wake up to the dark. As we wake up, we wake up to all of it. We wake to the joy and to the pain. We wake up to the injustices we've been inflicting upon ourselves, carrying in our own body, causing our disembodiment. As we wake up within, we wake up without. The injustices of the world are illuminated all the more fully.

Our hearts are vulnerable and tender by nature. Trauma puts a protective barrier around our hearts. As we learn it's not safe to love, to be vulnerable, to be open, our hearts close off. But as we heal, our awakened heart is activated, and we learn it's safe to love, to feel, to cry, to be intimate and vulnerable with ourselves and others. We navigate the world with an open heart, and the world heals in our presence because we offer love indiscriminately, and we all really need love—from self and from one another. The world needs your open heart.

But the world is full of suffering. There is hatred and violence, so much disparity and misfortune in the world. We may come to understand why we stayed asleep for so long. Waking up to all the suffering, all the hatred, makes us want to close down our hearts again. Yet the greatest injustice would be to experience a hardening of our own beautiful, tender, awakened heart.

My teacher Lama Tsultrim Allione says that we must preserve our bodhichitta, even in the darkest of times. The greatest injustice would be allowing someone who is openly and proudly hateful toward a particular group of people, for example, to harden our heart, to steal our bodhichitta, which the world so desperately needs. And if we were to close down our awakened heart, it would make us miserable, because having a tender, compassionate heart makes us feel alive. It allows for joy and connection—it relieves suffering.

When we were kids and people hurt us, we didn't know how to turn inward and be with our pain, to keep our hearts open and love ourselves all the same. But now we do. We don't have to let the ones who harm us harden our heart. That's what they want. The greatest act of resistance is to take care of your own tender, open heart. Shine the light of bodhichitta inward to the parts of you who are hurt.

✳

We are all awake; we've simply forgotten. Underneath the layers of pain and conditioning there is truth, and there is freedom. When we allow adversity to inform our motivation to heal, it transforms from something hindering into something alchemizing. We cannot control everything, and there are entire systems of oppression that must be disrupted shall collective freedom be attained. Yet, we have the power to initiate that collective process should we find the courage to look within and get to know the parts of us that block our own liberation.

The night of the Buddha's awakening, he could no longer run from himself. Sitting in silent meditation, determined, he was met again and again with his own inner demons who challenged him and tempted him to give up. Yet, moments before his enlightenment, sitting under the bodhi tree, he reached down and touched the earth, making the conscious decision to choose connection, to choose the present moment, and to choose freedom. Each day, in the easeful moments and the messy ones, we too have the opportunity to make that choice. It is my hope that this book has helped you reconnect to what is true, good, wise, and free within you. Know that the gates of nirvana are always open to you, should you choose to walk through. You were built for greatness. You have always been awake.

✳

EMBODIMENT PRACTICE:
NADI SHODHANA PRANAYAMA AND METTĀ MEDITATION

Embodiment Preparation

It's here friends, our final embodiment practice together. We'll move into a yoga pranayama called nadi shodhana, or alternate-nostril breathing, and then we'll close with a meditation that the Buddha taught, called mettā, or loving-kindness meditation.

Nadi Shodhana (Alternate-Nostril Breathing)

Figure 7.1 Merudanda Mudra

I invite you to find a comfortable, seated position.

I offer that we begin by taking several breaths and generating bodhichitta—a heart-centered intention to embody compassion and to be of service, to remove suffering within and out in the world.

We'll bring our hands to merudanda mudra, which is literally a thumbs-up position. Bring your hands into gentle fists, extending the thumbs. This is merudanda mudra, which supports the flow of pranayama, breath, or life-force energy throughout the body.

Bring the right hand in merudanda mudra to the right knee, and left hand in merudanda mudra to the left knee. Thumbs point up.

Take a couple of long, slow, deep, conscious breaths. Allow both the inhalations and the exhalations to come through the nose if that's comfortable. Find what works for you.

You might imagine your breath as a healing color, seeing that color enter and exit the body as you breathe in and breathe out.

Continue for several more cycles of breath.

Variation One
Begin to imagine that the breath enters up the right nostril on the inhalation, and out the left nostril on the exhalation. And then back up the left nostril on the inhalation, and out the right nostril on the exhalation. (Use the imagery of your healing color if it resonates.)

Allow your breath to slow down as you do this.

Practice this for several more cycles of breath.

You might choose to stay with this variation, doing exactly as you have been doing for another couple minutes. Or you might choose to try a second variation using your thumbs. If so . . .

Variation Two
After your next inhalation, pause. Lift your right thumb to your right nostril, gently pressing to close the nostril shut.

Exhale through the left nostril only. Pause. Inhale through the left nostril. Take your left thumb to your left nostril, gently pressing to close the nostril shut (now both nostrils are closed).

Remove your right thumb from your right nostril and exhale through the right nostril.

Inhale through the right nostril. Pause. Take your right thumb and gently close the right nostril.

Remove your left thumb from your left nostril and exhale through the left nostril. Pause. Inhale through the left nostril. Take your left thumb and gently close your left nostril. (Now both nostrils are closed.)

Remove your right thumb from your right nostril and exhale through the right nostril.

Continue until it feels complete for you—this could be another 10 seconds or another 10 minutes—it's your practice.

When it does feel complete, pause. Let go of the control of your breath. Notice.

If it feels meditative, you might stay here and meditate. If your body is needing movement, maybe begin to explore free movement or yoga asana. If you're ready to move on, anchor through your feet and open your eyes when you're ready.

Orient yourself to the space around you, and record your observations, curiosities, and intentions. When you're ready, I invite you to join me for mettā practice.

Mettā Meditation

As always, find a comfortable position for your body. If you wish, bring your palms to svabhava mudra by placing your hands over your heart, one palm over the other, and uniting the thumbs. Svabhava means "own-being." Placing the hands at the heart invites us to take refuge

Figure 7.2 Svabhava Mudra

within, and, as a bonus, it stimulates the vagus nerve and can bring comfort to our nervous system and all our many parts.

Allow yourself to get grounded, and when you are ready, invite yourself to connect to someone you find it easy to love. Imagine this person sitting across from you.

Look them in the eye and notice your body. Breathe.

When you feel ready, repeat these words silently or aloud, sending them to this person:

> May you be happy, may you be peaceful,
> May you be filled with loving-kindness.
> May you be free from suffering,
> May you feel free,
> May you love and be loved.

Pause. Notice your body. What's happening?

Breathe.

Send the words once more:

> May you be happy, may you be peaceful,
> May you be filled with loving-kindness.
> May you be free from suffering,
> May you feel free,
> May you love and be loved.

Notice your body. Allow the image of this person to dissolve.

Breathe.

Invite yourself to connect to someone (a person or group) you find it challenging to love. Imagine this person sitting across from you.

Look them in the eye and notice your body. Breathe.

When you feel ready, repeat these words silently or aloud, sending them to this person:

> May you be happy, may you be peaceful,
> May you be filled with loving-kindness.
> May you be free from suffering,
> May you feel free,
> May you love and be loved.

Pause. Notice your body. What's happening?

Breathe.

Send the words once more:

> May you be happy, may you be peaceful,
> May you be filled with loving-kindness.
> May you be free from suffering,
> May you feel free,
> May you love and be loved.

Notice your body. Allow the image of this person to dissolve.

Breathe.

Invite yourself to connect to your own body. Imagine yourself sitting across from you (remain playfully curious about the age/version of you that arrives).

Look into your own eyes and notice your body. Breathe.

When you feel ready, repeat these words silently or aloud, sending them to the version of you that's across from you:

> May you be happy, may you be peaceful,
> May you be filled with loving-kindness.
> May you be free from suffering,
> May you feel free,
> May you love and be loved.

Pause. Notice your body. What's happening?

Breathe.

Send the words once more:

May you be happy, may you be peaceful,
May you be filled with loving-kindness.
May you be free from suffering,
May you feel free,
May you love and be loved.

Notice your body. Allow the image of yourself to dissolve.

Connect inward to yourself this time. Turn your focus inward to your breath and body-mind.

When you're ready, gently direct these words inward:

May I be happy, may I be peaceful,
May I be filled with loving-kindness.
May I be free from suffering,
May I feel free,
May I love and be loved.

Pause. Notice your body. What's happening?

Breathe.

Send the words once more:

May I be happy, may I be peaceful,
May I be filled with loving-kindness.
May I be free from suffering,
May I feel free,
May I love and be loved.

Breathe. Witness.

For this final round, send the wishes outward to all beings everywhere, repeating these words:

> May all beings everywhere be happy, may all beings
>   everywhere be peaceful,
> May all beings everywhere be filled with loving-kindness.
> May all beings everywhere be free from suffering,
> May all beings everywhere feel free,
> May all beings everywhere love and be loved.

Breathe.

> May all beings everywhere be happy, may all beings
>   everywhere be peaceful,
> May all beings everywhere be filled with loving-kindness.
> May all beings everywhere be free from suffering,
> May all beings everywhere feel free,
> May all beings everywhere love and be loved.

Pause. Notice your body. What's happening?

Breathe.

In your own time, allow this practice to dissolve. Feel your feet against the earth. Send gratitude inward and out, if it feels right. Slowly, open your eyes.

FOLLOW-UP

Option 1: Take some time to journal or record, be in silent meditation, create art, move your body, whatever it feels like you need, after completing this practice. Honor what you need.

Option 2: How was it working with the person (or group) whom you found it hard to love? If you found yourself activated, experiencing any noticeable body sensations, thoughts, or feelings in relationship to this, you might return to the Befriending a Part practice at the end of Chapter Five, in order to be with any activation you're feeling in a loving way.

✳

Additional Embodiment Practice: Mettā for Parts

Connect to a particular part of you, emotion, thought, or physical sensation in your body, as you would for the Befriending a Part practice. Then imagine sending mettā to that part of you.

Additional Embodiment Practice: Mettā for Ancestors

Connect to an individual ancestor (whom you knew or didn't know), or a collective of ancestors. Then imagine sending them mettā.

CLOSING WITH INTENTION

Beautiful beings, we have arrived. I am deeply humbled and forever grateful that you have trusted me to guide you through this journey. There is so much that I wish for you, that I wish for this world.

I invite you to stay connected to the embodiment meditations in this book—these practices are meant to be lifelong sources of refuge for you along your healing journey. Take what resonates moment by moment. Leave what doesn't, until it does again. We are all always changing.

May you continue to turn toward your pain and bring it onto your path, looking inward and befriending the parts of you that need your care. May you experience more joy, more peace, more love, and more freedom in your life. May you walk embodied, supported, and knowing you belong here. May you continue to heal, evolve, and tap into your true nature more and more. And at times when you forget, may you quickly remember that you have always been whole, that you have always been awake.

As you awaken, may you help others wake up too.

I believe in you. I believe in your path.

May you be happy, may you be peaceful, may you be filled with loving-kindness. May you be free from suffering, may you feel free, may you love and be loved.

May the healing and benefits obtained by way of these words contribute to the liberation and awakening of all beings, living and nonliving, without exception.

Appendix A: Diaphragmatic Breath Tutorial

Deep, diaphragmatic breathing is at the foundation of many of the embodiment practices within this text. If breath work of this kind is new to you, or if you need a refresher, I'm offering here a yogic breath practice called ujjayi pranayama, or victorious breath. A brief background and history of yoga is provided at the end of Chapter Four, where you will also find several yoga asanas (postures) to help increase embodiment. Many of us find deep breathing calming to our nervous systems, but there are definitely people who are more activated than soothed by deep breathing. If this becomes your experience, please follow up with Appendix B for support.

*

I like to teach ujjayi pranayama in two parts. I invite you to find a comfortable seat, and we'll begin.

Ujjayi Pranayama: Victorious Breath

Find a comfortable position for your body, lying down, seated, or standing.

Ujjayi Preparation
I invite you to bring your hands into a comfortable position, joining them in your lap or resting them on your knees.

Allow your attention to travel to your breath. This is often most easily done by turning your attention to your abdomen, where you may more easily observe the breath moving in and out.

After several moments of observing the breath, begin to consciously deepen the breath. To do so, begin to inhale through your nose, <u>allowing your abdomen to inflate first and then your chest</u>.

As you exhale, allow the breath to leave through the mouth with a long, slow "haaa" sound (it's the sound you would make to fog up a pair of glasses). Let the breath release <u>out of the chest first, and then the abdomen</u>.

As you continue, try slowing the breath down, perhaps inhaling for a count of four or five, and exhaling for a count of four or five.

Practice for around 10 breath cycles (one inhalation and one exhalation together make one cycle), or as long as feels right for you.

Ujjayi Pranayama

To continue, inhale exactly as you did before, but <u>as you exhale, this time, keep your top and bottom lips sealed gently together</u>. You're still creating that whispery "haaa" sound from the throat as you exhale, but with the lips sealed, the breath actually leaves through the nose.

Listen to the oceanic sound created by your breath, if that feels soothing to you.

Continue breathing like this if you're finding this practice supportive.

Eventually, you might elongate the exhalation to be longer than the inhalation.

As you're breathing, notice your state of body–mind.

Continue this practice for as long as it feels right to you.

When it begins to feel complete, close with intention, maybe offering an affirmation or words of compassion inward.

Consciously exit this practice, pausing and noticing the body–mind–heart before moving or jumping into the next activity.

You might journal or record your observations with audio/video, drawing, music, dance, or whatever creative expression resonates with you right now.

Feel free to return to this practice often.

Appendix B: When the Breath Is Activating: A Resource

It is not uncommon for trauma survivors to be unsettled by pranayama (breath work) or focused breathing of any kind. What is a most powerful regulator of our nervous system can be an equally powerful dysregulator.

If focused breathing is activating for you rather than soothing, there is nothing wrong with you. The benefit of pranayama is that it can provide a shift in consciousness, and with this, it can open up space inside and allow trauma being held in the body to move through and out. But sometimes what comes up with breath work takes us outside of our window of tolerance, and we experience overwhelm. Creating an expansiveness in the body can be triggering for those whose systems use disembodiment as protection.

While it is necessary to allow the pain to surface in order to release it, we don't want to flood your system—that's not healing. If not today, in time, your system will evolve and breath work will become accessible. I have worked with countless beings who were initially too activated by pranayama to enjoy the practice, but who over time experienced a shift and the ability to soothe and settle their systems with pranayama.

Know that this is temporary. As you approach the embodiment practices in this book, and your system experiences some healing, you will eventually get to a place where pranayama is less activating.

*

Here are some things to do if you are activated by pranayama practice:

1. *Offer compassion inward for your experience.*

2. *Trust the process.*
3. *Go to Appendix C and use the containment practice, if any-thing that is too much, too fast, or too soon surfaces.*
4. *Approach the embodiment practices in this book with a focus on the physical sensations you feel, as opposed to a focus on the breath.*
5. *Befriend the activation.* Practices like the Befriending a Part meditation in Chapter Five will support you in working with the parts of you that are activated by focused breathing. (Please note: I recommend approaching the embodiment practices offered in this book in sequential order, but trust your instinct.)
6. *Try a twisted yoga pose.* Twists help to get both hemispheres of the brain online and are therefore helpful in settling your system.

    See Chapter Four, the embodiment practice Bringing Embodiment to Our Shut-Down Parts for guidance into a seated or reclined twist.
7. *Start with the inhalation.* As you begin to try pranayama practice again, try focusing on the inhalations. I've found that for many people it's the exhalation that's most activating. See if the inhalation feels accessible.

Extended resource: Here are some things to do if you're in a public yoga class and the breath focus is too activating:[1]

- Focus on the sounds you hear instead.
- Focus on any soothing aromas in the room.

- Focus on the textures you are touching (your mat, your clothes, the ground).
- Focus on sensations in the body.

Peace on your journey. You are exactly where you are supposed to be.

Appendix C: Containment Practice: When It's Too Much, Too Fast, Too Soon

As we approach the body, there will be times when what we experience overwhelms our system's level of readiness. If in experiential practice this occurs for you, this containment practice can help you settle your system or return it to baseline.

To begin, consciously find a comfortable position for your body, sitting, lying, or standing.

Imagine that next to you there is a container. It can be any type of container that you wish (a mason jar, a basket, etc.). Let the container have a lid such that when you close the lid, you can hear it close.

Take whatever arose that was too much, too fast, or too soon—the thoughts, emotions, sensations, images, memories—and slowly place them in the container one at a time.

Once everything is placed inside the container, imagine closing the lid. Hear the sound it makes when it closes.

Where would you like to consciously place this container? Maybe it's in your kitchen cupboard, maybe it's in the car trunk of a friend who lives far away, or maybe it stays right beside you.

I offer that you choose a place to intentionally place this container so that when you are ready to process what is in it, you know where to find it.

See an image of yourself placing the container there.

I invite you to come back to the present and practice grounding through the senses. Slowly look around and notice five things you see. Slowly note four places where your body touches another surface (like the chair, the floor). Mindfully notice three sounds that you hear. Note two scents that you smell. Notice one thing that you taste.

Check in and notice how you're doing. Move your body, journal, call a friend, rest, or do whatever feels most supportive right now.

Note: The container is not meant to be used as a means to repress the pain we are carrying. This book is all about turning toward our pain. If you find yourself using this practice frequently, if you find that you are consistently containing the same thing(s) again and again, or if you find that you are not returning to the container to work with what's in it, this is a sign that you could use the support of a licensed somatic therapist.

Inclusive Therapists, Psychology Today, Therapy for Black Girls, and Therapy for Black Men are a few of many online therapist directories that can help you locate a provider in your area. You can also visit the Internal Family Systems, Trauma-Conscious Yoga Institute, EMDR, Somatic Experiencing, or Hakomi Institute websites to find therapists trained in those specific models of somatic psychotherapy.

I encourage you to seek connection and outside support along your journey in addition to using this book. We are not designed to do this on our own. Peace to you.

Notes

CHAPTER ONE: BEYOND SURVIVAL

1 Shaheen, J., & Salzberg, S. (Hosts). (2022, April 27). Getting close to the terror with Ocean Vuong [Audio podcast]. In *Life As It Is, Tricycle: The Buddhist Review*. https://tricycle.org/podcast/ocean-vuong/

2 "White body supremacy" is a term coined by Resmaa Menakem for an institutionalized system that intentionally privileges people navigating the world in white bodies. This includes people who are racially white and can extend to those who are not racially white but who are white-presenting in appearance. "Cis-hetero-patriarchy" is a term used to exemplify the intersectionality of the patriarchy with ideologies of homophobia, transphobia, and heteronormativity.

3 Implicit memory is unconscious memory.

4 Throughout this text, at times you'll see the term "body–mind," a reflection of the inseparability of the body and mind and their ongoing influence on one another.

5 Wattanarong, K. (Director). (2017). *The life of the Buddha* [Film]. BBC/Discovery Channel.

6 Yetunde, P. A., & Giles, C. A. (Eds.) (2020). *Black and Buddhist: What Buddhism can teach us about race, resilience, transformation and freedom*. Shambala.

7 "Person of culture" is a term used by Resmaa Menakem, a synonym for "people of color," "BIPOC," or "people of the global majority" (PGM or GM).

8 Buddhism is not a singular construct. Since its spread, multiple schools and traditions of Buddhism have arisen in different parts of the world. In Tibetan Buddhism, or Vajrayana, there are also "groundwork instructions" that include the four contemplations or preliminaries in addition to the Four Noble Truths.

9 Beverly, F. (1980). *Joy and pain* [Song]. On *Joy and pain*. Capitol Records.

10 Chinnaiyan, K. (2018, September 18). Navarathri: An inner path to Shakti [MOOC lecture]. *Embodied Philosophy*. https://www.embodiedphilosophy.com/navarathri-an-inner-path-to-shakti/

11 Porges, S. W. (2011). *The polyvagal theory: Neurophysiological foundations of emotion, attachment, communication, self-regulation*. Norton.

CHAPTER TWO: THE ESSENCE OF EMPTINESS

1 Khyentse, D. (2007). *The heart of compassion: The thirty-seven verses on the practice of a bodhisattva* (Padmakara Translation Group, Trans.). Shambala.

2 To be activated is another way of saying "triggered."

3 Sending compassion to those activated by the breath.

4 Thrangu, K. (2003). *Pointing out the Dharmakaya*. Snow Lion.

5 Rotterdam, C., & Oosthuizen, P. (2017, April 27). Chöd: Intro talk [Video]. Skymind Programs and Teachings. YouTube. https://www.youtube.com/watch?v=lEEWQ8DD9Xk&t=168s

6 Edou, J. (1996). *Machig Labdrön and the foundations of Chöd*. Snow Lion.

7 *The Tibetan book of the dead* (F. Fremantle & C. Trungpa, Trans.). (2000). Shambala Classics.

8 Thrangu, 2003.

9 Somé, M. P. (1998). *The healing wisdom of Africa: Finding life purpose through nature, ritual, and community.* Penguin Putnam.
10 Thrangu, 2003.
11 Mindfulness practice is a direct teaching of the Buddha.
12 O'Brien, B. (2018, July 28). *Three turnings of the dharma wheel.* Learn Religions. https://www.learnreligions.com/three-turnings-of-the-dharma-wheel-450003

CHAPTER THREE: AWAKENING OUR COMPASSIONATE HEARTS

1 Dalai Lama & Cutter, H. (2020). *The art of happiness: A handbook for living.* Riverhead.
2 Buddhadharma is the term used to refer to the teachings of the Buddha.
3 Buddhist Library. (2020, May 30). Brother Phap Hai: Each moment only once [Video]. YouTube. https://www.youtube.com/watch?v=oqfhclPePSM
4 Alshami, A. M. (2019). Pain: Is it all in the brain or the heart? *Current Pain and Headache Reports, 23*, 88. https://doi.org/10.1007/s11916-019-0827-4
5 From *Entering the Way of the Bodhisattva: A New Translation and Contemporary Guide*, by Shantideva, translated by Khenpo David Karma Choephel. Copyright © 2021 by David Karma Choephel. Reprinted by arrangement with The Permissions Company, LLC on behalf of Shambhala Publications Inc., Boulder, CO, www.shambhala.com.
6 Karma literally means "action." It's the concept that every action has consequences of a similar kind, which, in turn, has further consequences, and so on. Karma can be understood as the cellular memory, held in our body–mind, that informs the ways we think, feel, and behave. Karma is released as nirvana is attained.
7 Somé, M. P. (1998). *The healing wisdom of Africa: Finding life purpose through nature, ritual, and community.* Penguin Putnam.
8 "Tibetan Buddhism" is an umbrella term to describe various Buddhist schools, formulated in Tibet, which all fall under the Mahayana tradition. This includes Vajrayana or tantric Buddhism.
9 The term "window of tolerance" was coined by Dr. Dan Siegel.
10 Salva Magaz. (2022, February 7). Lojong: Training the mind: Jetsün Khandro Rinpoche [Video]. YouTube. https://www.youtube.com/watch?v=WPJ-nHmOxEk&t=28s
11 Hannebohm, S. (2021, September 21). Radical friendship and tonglen practice with Kate Johnson [Audio podcast]. *The Lion's Roar Podcast.* https://www.lionsroar.com/radical-friendship-and-tonglen-practice-with-kate-johnson/
12 McLeod, K. (1987). Translator's introduction. In J. Kongtrul, *The great path of awakening: The classic guide to lojong, a Tibetan Buddhist practice for cultivating the heart of compassion.* Shambhala Classics.
13 Thepostarchive. (2016, January 17). "The Negro in American culture" a group discussion (Baldwin, Hughes, Hansberry, Capouya, Kazin) [Video]. YouTube. https://www.youtube.com/watch?v=jNpitdJSXWY
14 Owens, L. R. (2020). *Love and rage: The path of liberation through anger.* North Atlantic.

CHAPTER FOUR: WIRED FOR AWAKENING

1 Dana, D. (2021). *Anchored: How to befriend your nervous system using polyvagal theory.* Sounds True.
2 Siegel, D. J. (1999). *The developing mind: How relationships and the brain interact to shape who we are.* Guilford.

3   Menakem, R. (2017). *My grandmother's hands: Racialized trauma and the pathway to mending our hearts and bodies.* Central Recovery Press.

4   Kolacz, J., Kovacic, K. K., & Porges, S. W. (2019). Traumatic stress and the autonomic brain-gut connection in development: Polyvagal theory as an integrative framework for psychosocial and gastrointestinal pathology. *Developmental Psychobiology, 61*(5), 796–809.

5   Porges, S. W., & Dana, D. (2018). *Clinical applications of the polyvagal theory: The emergence of polyvagal-informed therapies.* Norton.

6   Dana, D. (2020). *Polyvagal flip chart: Understanding the science of safety.* Norton.

7   Porges, S. W. (1998). Love: An emergent property of the mammalian autonomic nervous system. *Psychoneuroendocrinology, 23*(8), 837–861. https://doi.org/10.1016/S0306-4530(98)00057-2

8   Porges, S. W. (2011). *The polyvagal theory: Neurophysiological foundations of emotion, attachment, communication, self-regulation.* Norton.

9   Porges, S. W. (1995). Orienting in a defensive world: Mammalian modifications of our evolutionary heritage: A polyvagal theory. *Psychophysiology, 32*(4), 301–318. https://doi.org/10.1111/j.1469-8986.1995.tb01213.x

10 Dana, D. (2015). A beginner's guide to polyvagal theory. Resources. Deb Dana's Rhythm of Regulation. https://www.rhythmofregulation.com/resources

11 Dana, D. (2018). *Polyvagal theory in therapy: Engaging the rhythm of regulation.* Norton.

12 Henriques, A., & Shull, T. (Host). (2020, July 25). Polyvagal meets IFS: A talk with Deb Dana [Audio podcast]. IFS Talks. https://internalfamilysystems.pt/multimedia/webinars/polyvagal-meets-ifs-talk-deb-dana

13 Another way to conceptualize this is that the ego is trying to mobilize us back up to ventral.

14 Levine, P. A. (1997). *Waking the tiger: Healing trauma.* North Atlantic.

15 Schwartz, R. (n.d.). Video 1: How to work with the inner voice of shame [MOOC lecture]. In *How to work with shame.* National Institute for the Clinical Application of Behavioral Medicine. https://www.nicabm.com

16 Porges, S. W. (n.d.). Video 3: Part 1: How shame triggers the body's shut-down response [MOOC lecture]. In *How to work with shame.* National Institute for the Clinical Application of Behavioral Medicine. https://www.nicabm.com

CHAPTER FIVE: BEFRIENDING WHAT AILS US

1   Rinchen, S. (1998). *The six perfections* (R. Sonam, Trans.). Snow Lion.

2   Hannebohm, S. (2022, June 25). Wisdom and suffering with Brother Phap Hai [Audio podcast]. *The Lion's Roar Podcast.* https://www.lionsroar.com/the-lions-roar-podcast-wisdom-and-suffering-with-brother-phap-hai/

3   Edou, J. (1996). *Machig Labdrön and the foundations of Chöd.* Snow Lion. Allione, T. (2008). *Feeding your demons: Ancient wisdom for resolving inner conflict.* Little Brown.

4   Anderson, F. G. (2021). *Transcending trauma: Healing complex PTSD with internal family systems therapy.* PESI.

5   Schwartz, R. C., & Sweezy, M. (2020). *Internal family systems therapy* (2nd ed.). Guilford.

6   Schwartz, R. (2008). *You are the one you've been waiting for: Bringing courageous love to intimate relationships.* Trailhead.

7   Krause, P., Herbine-Blank, T., & Schwartz, R. (2018). IFS online circle: Foundations of the IFS model [MOOC lecture]. IFS Institute. https://ifs-institute.com/

8   To code-switch is to change how we talk in an attempt to avoid discrimination. "Global majority" is another term for Black, Indigenous, and People of Color (BIPOC), which emphasizes that BIPOC folx are not the minority but are actually the majority on a global scale.

CHAPTER SIX: TRANSFORMING THE LEGACY

1   Hanh, T. N. (2006). *Present Moment Wonderful Moment: Mindfulness Versus for Daily Living.* Parallax Press.
2   Lipton, B., & Bhaerman, S. (2010). *Spontaneous evolution: Our positive future and a way to get there from here.* Hay House.
3   Wolynn, M. (2017). *It didn't start with you: How inherited family trauma shapes who we are and how to break the cycle.* Penguin.
4   Perman, D. (2004). Interview with Dr. Bruce Lipton. *Pathways to Family Wellness,* no. 1. https://pathwaystofamilywellness.org/New-Edge-Science/an-interview-with-dr -bruce-lipton.html
5   Gustafson, C. (2017). Bruce Lipton, PhD: The jump from cell culture to consciousness. *Integrative Medicine: A Clinician's Journal, 16*(6), 44–50.
6   Lipton, B. (1997). The biology of nurturing: The impact of maternal emotions on genetic development: A conversation with Michael Mendizza. *Touch the Future.* https:// ttfuture.org/files/2/members/int_lipton.pdf
7   Lipton, 1997.
8   Wolynn, M. (2017). *It didn't start with you: How inherited family trauma shapes who we are and how to break the cycle.* Penguin.
9   Siegel, D. J. (2010). *The mindful therapist: A clinician's guide to mindsight and neural integration.* Norton.
10 Parnell, L. (2013). *Attachment-focused EMDR: Healing relational trauma.* Norton.
11 Duvernay, A. (Director). (2016). *13th: From slave to criminal with one amendment* [Film]. Kandoo Films.
12 Kendi, I. X. (2016). *Stamped from the beginning: The definitive history of racist ideas in America.* Bold Type.

CHAPTER SEVEN: SEVERING OUR ATTACHMENT TO SUFFERING

1   Bhumisparsha. (2022, May 30). Medicine Buddha w/ Lama Rod Owens [MOO]. https://www.crowdcast.io/e/medicine-buddha-lama-rod/register
2   Williams, A. K. (2000). *Being Black: Zen and the art of living with fearlessness and grace.* Penguin.
3   Rinpoche, C. T. (2003). *Parting from the four attachments: A commentary on Jetsun Drakpa Gyaltsen's song of experience on mind training and the view.* Snow Lion.
4   Edou, J. (1996). *Machig Labdrön and the Foundations of Chöd.* Snow Lion.
5   Gates, R. (2015). *Meditations on intention and being: Daily reflections on the path of yoga, mindfulness, and compassion.* Anchor.
6   SF Dharma Collective. (2020, August 28). Mind training: Cultivating compassion and insight. Lojong slogans: Self-liberate the antidote [Video]. YouTube. https://www .youtube.com/watch?v=exV7jtYz5BU&t=3159s

APPENDIX B: WHEN THE BREATH IS ACTIVATING

1   Gessel, N. (2018, June 28). Trauma-informed yoga: When the breath acts as a trigger. *Elephant Journal.* https://www.elephantjournal.com/2018/06/trauma-informed-yoga -when-the-breath-acts-as-a-trigger/

Index

Index

About the Author

Nityda Gessel is a licensed somatic psychotherapist, trauma specialist, yoga teacher and educator, mother, and heart-centered activist. Nityda is the founder of the Trauma-Conscious Yoga Institute, devoted to equity and increasing access to embodied, trauma-informed education and healing, while honoring yoga's roots and decolonizing the practice in the West. Nityda is the creator of The Trauma-Conscious Yoga Method[SM], a holistic healing modality that unites the wisdom of yoga and Buddhism with somatic psychotherapeutic practices. Nityda's integrative work over the past two decades has significantly contributed to the synthesis of the mental health and yoga/embodiment professions. Nityda founded the Trauma-Conscious Equity Foundation to narrow the health disparity gap between served and underserved communities by providing funding for BIPOC and LGBTQIA+ mental health professionals to receive yoga and somatic training. For you, Nityda wishes a life of joy, freedom, and peace.